6 Weeks to Happy

The Ultimate Roadmap
To Retrain Your Brain
For Better Health, Greater Abundance,
And Long Lasting Happiness

BY ZAHRA KARSAN,

FOUNDER & CEO GETZENd

6 Weeks to Happy

The Ultimate Roadmap to Retrain Your Brain for Better Health, Greater Abundance, and Long-Lasting Happiness

ISBN-13: 978-0-578-95807-1

WHAT OTHERS ARE SAYING ABOUT "6 WEEKS TO HAPPY"

In her new book, renowned writer, coach and speaker, Zahra Karsan, provides a new insight on how to rewire your brain to restore our more natural calm state. Be prepared to create new neural connections of positivity, self-love and meaning. An easy read and a must read for all wanting to raise their self-awareness and vibrations, and for those wanting to live a happier and meaningful life.

-Chairman, Rekhi Centre For the Science of Happiness Indian Institute of Technology, Kharagpur, India

"I love the ultimate roadmap and guidance that is so needed these days to achieve our optimal state in order to live fully. Zahra has been able to write a book that can evolve yourself and the greater good. Brilliant. A must read which we can embed into our lives, and then share"

- **Luis Gallardo:** Founder & President, World Happiness Foundation
https://worldhappiness.foundation

It is rare that an author writes a transformative guide from one's own experience both personally and as a success coach. This makes Zahra's book a powerful contribution to the ailing world. Her 6 Week R.E.W.I.R.E System™ alters prerecorded information in the subconsciousness and enables you to become a happier and more fulfilled soul. I congratulate Zahra for this unique life-changing guidebook. Please take advantage of it and seek to evolve as a greater human being.

-**Saamdu Chetri,** Founding member and Former Executive Director of Gross National Happiness Centre Bhutan, Author & Visiting Professor, Rekhi Centre of Excellence for the Science of Happiness, IIT Kharagpur, India
http://saamduchetri.com

Zahra is a lighthouse and a powerhouse with a gentle soul. The book 6 Weeks to Happy is, in essence, a great guide to self-compassion in action with Zahra as your guide. When I work with organizations and leaders on Organizational Happiness *and* The Happiness Sweet Spot *as a motor for success,* Compassion in Action *is an essential pillar. The fundamental platform for cultivating a culture of compassionate leadership in organizations is awareness and self-compassion for every leader. I don't think you can have real leadership without compassion. Here is a practical guide and a roadmap to create that fundamental awareness. I love how Zahra shares her personal stories and insights. And the focus on energy and flow is great I think. Highly recommended.*

-**Lars Kure Juul** Author of the #1 International Bestseller "*Organizational Happiness*", Founder and CVO of Motivational Landscape

Zahra has taken her richly lived personal and professional experience as well as her deep study of different cultural understandings of happiness to offer this highly practical, concise, and precise roadmap towards happiness! Practicing the many valuable tools in this book will help you to rewire your brain towards practices that will allow you to be healthier and happier, whatever your starting point may be. Zahra's suggested approach is powerful and easy to follow!
As someone who has been immersed in the field of human flourishing, thanks to my role as the Founding Director of the University for Peace, established by the General Assembly of the United Nations, Zahra has been a distinguished speaker in our annual Gross Global Happiness Summit. She touched people through her presentation there and I'm delighted that her book will now reach a much wider audience!

-**Mohit Mukherjee,** Founding Director, UPEACE Centre for Executive Education

www.centre.upeace.org

Bringing together many fields of study in the search for happiness and well-being, Zahra has pulled together a clear set of tools to help retrain your brain and body back to its natural state of calm. You'll discover the why and how of happiness that has eluded so many of us for so long. Going deeper into self-healing, you'll learn the techniques to better understand yourself and what you really need to feel your best. Finding peace as we live busy and pro-

ductive lives never felt possible before but it does now. Follow this easy 6-week road to happiness and you will find better health, a profound sense of inner peace and deeper connection with yourself, with others and with the world around you.

-**Raj Raghunathan, Ph.D.**, Author of '*If You're so Smart, Why Aren't You Happy?*
Centennial Professor of Business, McCombs School of Business, The University of Texas at Austin
www.happysmarts.com

In 6 Weeks to Happy, *Zahra Karsan provides a simple happiness system that WORKS. She's summarized the science and created practical tools to REWIRE your brain, body, spirit and soul for calm, peace, joy, and purpose. Read this book and you'll immediately not only feel better but be on the path to living an extraordinary life, better than you ever imagined!*

-**Carin Rockind,** Professor of Applied Positive Psychology at The Flourishing Center, Speaker and Coach, Founder & Host of the Purpose Girl Podcast
www.carinrockind.com

It is with tremendous pride and a happy heart that I have both the honor and the privilege in which to provide my book endorsement to Zahra Karsan on her latest and greatest body of work thus far - 6 Weeks to Happy.
I have immense respect for Zahra and all that she continues to tirelessly do within the realm of inspiring others. Zahra is internationally recognized and globally sought out for her multitude of dynamic skills and talents as it relates to her passion for raising the collective consciousness for all of humanity.
Zahra is quite notably one of the top-ranked authentic messengers for the happiness narrative. This is a woman who is conscientious and deliberately intentional with living in her own happiness as an evolved, self-empowered human being. Zahra's contributions to the overall collective and for the benefit of all are both innumerable and immeasurable! I, for one, am profoundly impacted and consistently enlightened by Zahra!
6 Weeks to Happy is not only a must-read book...it is the gift that keeps on giving. I highly recommend that this book be on the bedside table of those who are genuinely seeking inner bliss, emotional equilibrium, and should often be re-read by those who are committed to nurturing, cultivating and preserving

their inward happiness journey! Your current, daily and future self will thank you!

-**Lisa McDonald,** Radio Host of Living Fearlessly with Lisa McDonald and Member of Forbes Coaches Council LivingFearlesslyWithLisa.Com

Zahra skillfully guides us through the groundbreaking 6 Week RE.W.I.R.E. System™ that will benefit your spiritual, mental, emotional and physical bodies in a way that is truly life transforming and soul feeding. Learn the techniques and practical strategies you need to awaken your inner calm and activate your inner coach from a world class success coach. Essential reading for anyone interested in optimal well-being, true happiness and long-lasting peace. Highly recommend!!

-**Peggy Farmer, Ph.D.,** Founder & CEO, Self Mastery International Author of "Exploratory Surgery of the Soul, A Journey to Self Mastery" www.selfmasteryintl.com

This is music to my ears! 6 Weeks to Happy is a pathway to the most passionate yearning of human beings – the attainment of happiness – across time and space. This journey inward, this call to return to our native source in our search for happiness, honors the vital claims of the many elements that make us who we are – our physical, social, emotional, spiritual dimensions. Zahra Karsan dives deep into the inner self and presents a roadmap to discover true joy and abundance. I commend Ms Karsan for this compelling invitation to the ultimate.

-**Thakur S Powdyel,** Former Minister of Education, Royal Government of Bhutan, Author of My Green School; As I Am, So Is My Nation; & Right of Vision & Occasional Views

TABLE OF CONTENTS

DEDICATION

To LOVE

Because that's all there is.

In the end, you realize that to find the ultimate peace, the entire journey is about discovering ourselves, who we are meant to be in this world, how to be more loving, kind and compassionate toward ourselves and others. We learn the interconnectedness of all things and the only way to this place is to honor our authentic selves, to be okay with our imperfections and to have the courage to heal and love anyway. Sometimes the journey is arduous, but unless we are willing to find our way back to wholeness, life will always seem disconnected and fractured. It is only in learning to slow down, lean into healing and surrender ourselves entirely, that we find our true strength, self-love, and the deep connection we all seek.

PART I:

STEP INTO YOUR HAPPINESS

My business clients come to me with all manner of requests—boost their productivity, increase their sales performance, increase revenue, advance their leadership capabilities, and build stronger teams. But whether global executives or small-shop creatives, their latest desire alone won't bring them the happiness they seek because, at the end of the day, we're human beings. And most of these processes and outcomes can forget that human element. We can't easily achieve better sales, greater wealth, improved health, and a happier, more fulfilled life just by focusing on a business goal alone to the detriment of everything else in our lives because that's not how we're wired. How do I know? I chased happiness until it made me miserable, which set me on a more than twenty-year study of psychology, self-analysis, positive psychology, neuroscience and happiness.

Back in the day, I thought I finally reached a wonderful point in my career. I was a top management consultant and trusted advisor to global executives. CEOs hired me when multi-million dollar projects had gone off the rails or when their company needed restructuring. I was an under-the-radar hired gun, known for her grit and ability to deliver. I loved the high energy, powerful position and became a master of strategy and execution. I thrived and got a high from a job well done. When CEOs asked for me directly, the ultimate accolade, I knew I'd done well at my job and soon earned a reputation of delivering challenging projects in tricky situations. I didn't need public awards or recognition.

But, even with all my professional success, all wasn't well in my world. My brief marriage was on the rocks. There was tension in my family relationships, sleepless nights, and total exhaustion. With my stress level at an all-time high. I began to crack under the pressure. My physical body was a tightly wound mess of stress and anxiety. My mental body was exhausted. My emotional body was completely depleted. And I ignored my spiritual body entirely. Oh, did I mention we have 4 bodies?

Our Four Bodies

When most people think of health, they only consider their physical bodies. While the physical body is important, it's only one aspect of ourselves. We need to acknowledge other factors that contribute to our overall well-being. If we want a vibrant, healthy life, we need to start paying attention to our spiritual, mental, and emotional bodies, too. We are energetic beings and yet we ignore these other important aspects of ourselves. This shows up when we spend time with the wrong groups of people that drain us, engage in activities that don't always restore, support and console us, even when we need that moment to look after ourselves instead.

Most ancient cultures talked about the connection between body, mind, and spirit and recognized that each composed a part of the whole. Now, integrative medicine and health psychology are beginning to recognize that health is influenced not only by the physical body but the spiritual, mental, and emotional bodies, too. Even positive psychology has applications for looking after each of the four bodies with a view that they each contribute to our overall happiness and sense of wellbeing. Here's a rundown of the four bodies and why you need to keep them balanced and in harmony.

The 4 Bodies of Self

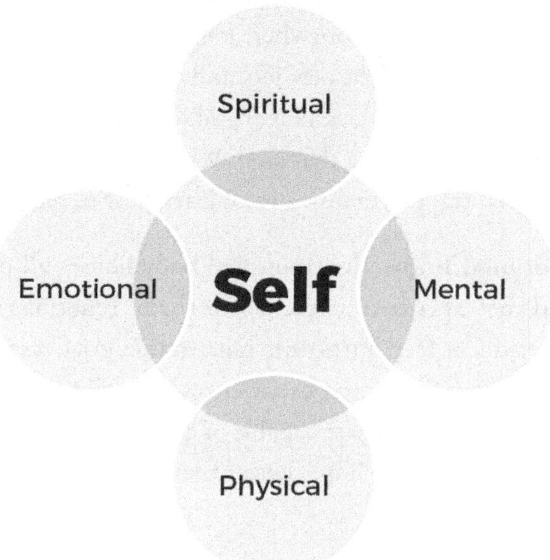

The Spiritual Body. The spiritual body is your connection to energy. Whatever works for you. If your connection to energy resonates in religion and spirituality, then think of it in those terms. For others, this has to do with quantum energy. Whichever way you choose to view the source of your energy is perfect.

> Energy trickles down from the spiritual body, from source, or the universe and first enters into the mental body. To fully access the spiritual aspect of your being, maintain a daily practice that keeps this connection open. If a blockage occurs, energy and information are unable to flow freely from the spiritual body down through the mental, emotional, and physical bodies… …To be in a state of harmony between each of the layers of our being, we need to develop our intuition and spirituality as much as we do our mind, emotions, and muscles to create a solid physical foundation.[1]

The Mental Body. This holds your thoughts, beliefs, values, desires and goals and critical thinking. As energy flows from the mental to the emotional body, it runs into past negative emotions and significant life events and so changes course from where it might like to flow. For example, we set a goal for achieving that new job, and as we think of claiming that position, we run into old patterns of fear and self-doubt which may hinder, or even stop us from achieving that goal. We must develop self-awareness of old patterns and trapped emotions and learn how to self-regulate.

The Emotional Body. The emotional body houses all past negative emotions and the experiences attached to them. Emotions can keep us stuck—anger, sadness, fear, hurt, guilt, rage, shame, grief, resentment. This is where we add meaning to past experiences and store these moments as memories. It is also where we are capable of clearing those stuck pathways to make room for joy, peace, hope, love, passion and fulfillment to reside, among others.

This is where past emotions impact our future in the way of anxiety and worry. When there is past trauma or unhealed upset, thoughts from the mental body will generate emotional stress that affects the physical body. A person with overwhelming stress (and we are all stressed) will, at some point, experience physical symptoms because of the mind-body connection, sometimes very serious physical symptoms. This is why we need to start to look after the mental and emotional bodies, develop emotional intelligence and learn how to regulate ourselves so we can stay in balance. This has a positive impact on our physical body and brings us into a healthier state overall. Later in this book, you will have an opportunity to go deeper and learn to develop a daily practice to keep all four bodies finely tuned and in harmony.

The Physical Body. This is your tangible body, the one we can see and is a reflection of how all four bodies are doing. Besides providing the musculoskeletal structure and vital tissues and organs that carry us through life, it also acts as a gauge for how we are doing. If we are not properly managing stress and our four-body system, oftentimes our physical bodies will give us warning signs—auto-immune disorders, chronic pain, inflammation, high blood pressure and dis-EASE. While exercise and healthy eating are needed to look after the physical body, we also need to manage stress in the other bodies to keep the physical body in peak health.

Stress triggers the fight-or-flight response. We evolved with this survival mechanism, and it's hard-wired into our DNA. It is how our bodies prepare to respond to potentially life-threatening events. When this response is triggered repeatedly, it creates wear and tear on the physical body.

I remember one day that illustrates this flight-or-flight response perfectly. I walked quickly to the office kitchen for a cup of coffee. It occurred to me that I did most things quickly, even breathing. Then it hit me. I was barely breathing. But, why? As I sat with that question, I became aware of the incredible amount of tension in my neck and shoulders. My chest was so tight I couldn't breathe deeply. I'd been sprinting for so long, I forgot how to slow down long enough to enjoy a walk or a cup of coffee. My lifestyle had crept into my physical body.

At that moment of realization, I ran into my boss. He asked me if I had a few minutes, which usually meant something was about to change. When he suddenly put my big project on hold, my thoughts raced. *What priorities shifted? Am I being moved to another project? Is my project being postponed?* Potentially the hold could've meant that all the work I'd done might have been for nothing. Now, this is normal in the corporate world, but it still FEELS like a lot of work and stress just gets thrown out the window, which is hard to process. Sure enough, my project was put on hold.

I'm not sure if it was the news that my work and my team's work was about to be pushed aside or the realization that I might be able to relax for a few weeks, but I suddenly became very emotional. All that stress bubbled up inside and I just felt the tears start streaming down my face and onto the floor of my boss's office. He just looked at me, wide-eyed. We both sat there, shocked. I'd NEVER lost my cool. I'd betrayed my laser-focus and "calm under pressure" composure. There we were, both of us wondering how to respond. I was known for my professionalism and there it was... evaporating in a pile of tears.

I took a moment to collect myself and apologized, totally embarrassed. I will never forget his support and compassion in that moment.

He just calmly said, "It's ok, tell me what's going on."

I explained how stressed I'd been in my personal life and asked if I could take a week off.

He just looked at me and said, "I'm so sorry to hear that you've been going through so much. You go do what you need. Your health comes first. Your life comes first. Work will always be here. Take all the time you need. We will be here when you're ready to come back. I think you should just take as much time as you need."

I sighed and felt complete relief. I'd pushed myself so hard for so long! I'd pushed my team hard. Until they pushed back and revolted, saying my demands were too much. Before my boss's invitation gave me time to regroup, it didn't even occur to me that there might be a different way to operate in business and in the world. A way that didn't require me to sprint all day, every day. But thanks to my team's mutiny, my crumbling health, and my unhappiness, the stress forced me to look for another way.

I had no idea what to think or do with this unexpected time off, but I knew something needed to change. After a couple of days of deep sleep, I woke up feeling a bit more like myself. I poured a big mug of coffee and sat on the couch, staring out at the lake outside my living room window. My whole body felt frazzled. I sat there stunned, wondering how long I'd been living this way, on auto-pilot, running a marathon with no finish line.

There has to be more than this, I thought. *This. Is. Not. Working.* While I wasn't sure what was missing, I knew this lifestyle wasn't how I was meant to live. I'd read all the right books on what separates successful people from the rest of the population. I thought these things would give me purpose and therefore make me happy. They didn't, because, again, human beings aren't wired that way.

Where Happiness Lives

I searched outside the bounds of conventional wisdom about happiness and began reading books on self-analysis, positive psychology, and mindfulness. In their pages, I discovered common themes about how to live a happier, more balanced life through mindfulness, practicing gratitude, and positive thinking. When my personal life imploded I reluctantly and pessimistically (trust me, when I say that) began practicing meditation. I needed a moment of peace to hear myself think again. Not easy for this former, tightly-wound Type A personality.

I just started one day and said to myself, "Well, you have more than twenty years of research in psychology, self-analysis, positive psychology, and the study of happiness. You have all the tools you could possibly need to live a happier, more peaceful life. It's certainly worth a try to sit quietly, and just try to find some calm. I didn't even know where to start. I just knew I was tired of feeling anxious, stressed and unhappy. I was tired of feeling *tired*. Then a voice inside me said, *what do you want to feel instead?* Just start with that. I thought to myself, *I want to feel peaceful, happy and calm again*. So that's how it began.

I focused on just three feelings and breathed them in until my body vibrated with them—peaceful, happy, calm. This is all I did. The process only lasted five to seven minutes at first, then it expanded to ten and fifteen minutes. Soon it was the best part of my day. It became this uninterrupted moment where the world disappeared,—all the demands, the bills, everything, and I got to just be in this space where I really was peaceful, feeling happy, so relaxed, and so very calm. It felt like a vacation.

Soon I was able to actually picture moments where I first arrived on holiday, and the sun was shining on me, and my feet first felt the warm sand beneath my toes. This brought me into such a state of utter relaxation. After doing this for a few weeks, I felt so good that the feeling lasted throughout the day! So I said, ok, what's next?

This moment of meditation naturally expanded into a visualization where all the areas of my life were going beautifully. After focusing on what I wanted to FEEL, I would picture myself in perfect health, with my future love, in my social circle, in my relationships, with my family, at work, and my life feeling joyful and filled with adventure, abundance, excitement and freedom. That's it. That's how I started.

After just a few weeks of doing this practice, I felt so much lighter! My breathing was more relaxed. Things didn't upset me as easily. I was laughing more. I. Just. Felt. BETTER. Life felt easier. I didn't know it at the time, but I'd stumbled onto a magic formula, which was a short, daily practice, and it transformed my life! This was the basis of what was to become part of **The R.E.W.I.R.E System™**.

I felt a profound shift—calmer, more sure of myself—and so much happier, but, I also felt a bit conflicted. On the outside, I was a high-powered corporate player, but on the inside, I'd become lighter. I couldn't really share my experience with my colleagues. No one at work talked about meditation or mindfulness. And if I mentioned gratitude, they looked at me like they desperately wanted to change the subject—I was a total badass wanting to talk about counting the daisies? No way.

So I kept my new practices, my shift, and my happiness to myself for a while. Still, friends noticed. The world noticed. People received me so much more warmly and differently—like they couldn't wait to meet me. I began to master the art of creating a happy and abundant life. Amazing things like more opportunities, money, friendships and deepening relationships began showing up in my life. Everyone who knew me then can tell you the same. My happiness helped me build the life of my dreams! And then

I realized, *this is what I want to do.* I need to study everything I can and do all the research necessary, so I can help others do the same. This is my soul's purpose.

So I expanded my research to try to uncover what has us stuck in old emotions and why we keep choosing the wrong things, the wrong partner, the wrong lifestyle. I began studying many fields of expertise that explored the subconscious and the processing of emotions and life events, so I could learn how to help people move beyond their fear and doubt and create a new version of themselves. I studied Neurolinguistic Programming and Hypnotherapy at a Master level, so I could really uncover the mechanics of the subconscious and then learn how to dismantle old patterns and put in place new, healthier habits.

I studied neuroscience because I wanted to understand how the brain perceives life events, how it stores and recalls memories and emotions. I needed to understand optimal brain health and which neurochemicals make us feel good or bad and how to regulate them. I then studied applied positive psychology, to understand how to progress into happiness and wellbeing.

To quote one of the founders of Positive Psychology, Dr. Christopher Peterson, "Positive Psychology is about helping people move north of neutral."

In effect, I was trying to understand where happiness lives.

After all my studies, I realized there's no easy answer. Happiness is about more than making peace with the past and overcoming fear and doubt. It's about learning about ourselves and understanding how to look after and align our four bodies so we can be in harmony. Like the perfect melody, this somehow enables us to *vibrate* at the level of happiness.

The good news is you don't have to take the 30 years I did to explore and unpack where happiness lives—you can find it in six weeks! I gave my system the acronym **R.E.W.I.R.E** and began putting it into practice in my own life and in the lives of my clients. It distills all of my research and results into a groundbreaking, easy, transformative system to discover happiness by learning and implementing the necessary tools for long-lasting change—better health, greater abundance, more joy, less stress and greater happiness. The best part? Once you have these tools, you get to keep them for life.

Why six weeks? One of the biggest and most useful discoveries of the last several decades has been that brain plasticity (known as "neuroplasticity") lasts throughout our lives. Neuroplasticity describes how the brain can adapt to changes in an individual's environment by forming new neural connections over time. Over time, performing the same set of actions repeatedly fires off the same neural circuit, strengthening the synaptic connections and that neural circuit begins to wire together. Therefore, the rewired human brain is able to adapt, master new skills, store memories and information, and even recover after a traumatic brain injury. Neuroplasticity also allows us to evolve our actions and modify our behavior so that we can live more powerfully, with ease.[2]

This means our brains can make new connections and change patterned-thinking no matter our age. Even more exciting – it typically takes only six weeks of practice for a newly formed neural pathway to become the brain's neural pathway of choice. In these pages, I will present important scientific evidence to show how we can **R.E.W.I.R.E.** and retrain our brains for lasting change.

The Why And How of Happiness

While I built my successful performance and leadership consulting firm, I also formalized my studies in happiness. I became certified at a master's level in Neurolinguistic Programming (NLP) and hypnotherapy, so I could better understand the subconscious and how to move past our limitations. I completed a certificate in neuroscience to understand optimal brain health. I also formalized my training in applied positive psychology, the study of wellbeing and vitality.

After stumbling into a short morning routine that changed my life, I wanted to dissect it and understand how and why incorporating simple practices into my daily routine created such a big shift in every aspect of my life. I wanted to understand all the science and research that explained why and how this transformation occurred. And I wanted to develop a simple, easy-to-follow program to help others—especially my clients—make that shift for themselves, so they could live better, feel better, and be happier at their core.

Through my studies, I came to see why happiness is always just out of reach for most of us. I also started to understand the physiology and psychology of how the shift toward happiness occurs. So often in our culture, we place all our value on professional capabilities and technical skills, which are wonderful things. But we forget about protecting and nurturing the human being within. We forget, or some of us don't even know, how to develop and tend to what I call critical life skills such as self-esteem and emotional resilience. We don't make time to understand our personal needs. In fact, we are never really asked as we grow up, what our needs are and what, specifically, makes us happy! So is it any wonder that no matter what we achieve, no matter how many brass rings we grab, so many of us are left feeling unfulfilled and unhappy?

In the corporate world, we're always defining goals, creating plans, and then measuring our success. In our personal lives, we might set a goal for "happiness." Yet, we don't know how to make a plan to achieve it because we don't know what happiness means for us. Happiness isn't a thing we own or achieve. It's a state of being that must be cultivated inside. Just because we didn't learn how to cultivate it when we were younger, doesn't mean it's too late to train our brains to achieve it now.

R.E.W.I.R.E. for Happiness in 6 Weeks

The six-week **R.E.W.I.R.E. System**™ features three tools each week, designed to help you understand the benefits and science behind each tool and how their implementation will bring more happiness to your life. This proven method aligns the four bodies—spiritual, mental, emotional and physical—bringing them into harmony, so you can *vibrate* at the level of happiness.

Week 1—**Relax & Quiet the Mind**—build self-awareness and learn to quiet the voices in your head and retrain your body back to calm. You'll get off the hamster wheel of life and learn how to be more present. Out of survival mode, you can access a more peaceful and productive state of mind.

Week 2—**Eliminate the Noise**—learn Emotional Intelligence and how to regulate your energy for a more fun and fulfilling life.

Week 3—**What Do You Need?**—understand your unique core needs and how you can make small adjustments in your life to ensure your needs are met more often. This will lead to a more exciting and joyous life.

Week 4—**Imagine & Visualize a new future**—tap into your deepest values and redesign a life that really lights you up.

Week 5—**Repeat & Rewire**—to rewire our brains, we need to create a new daily practice so that we think, feel and act in a new way. In this module, you'll learn how to do this for yourself so you can have a life you truly love.

Week 6—**Elevate & Expand**—just when you think you have a powerful new vision for your life, we will elevate that and create an even bigger and brighter future for you—one where you are truly thriving!

Within the first few weeks of working on this plan, clients often report feeling lighter. By week four, they're moving through their lives with more ease, less upset and tension, and living with greater joy. By week six, the thought patterns they developed through the program's practices and exercises are taking root, becoming natural where happiness has become a habit.

Based on my clients' successes, as well as how my life has transformed for the better, I knew I had to get The R.E.W.I.R.E. System™ to a broader audience. So I decided to write this book. The book is organized to take you through a six-week happiness transformation with precise explanations, easy-to-follow, fun exercises, and regular practices. I recommend you read through the book completely once, without doing the exercises. Then, each week, read the text and work through the corresponding practices and exercises. You'll also get to gauge how you're doing each week and throughout the program by rating yourself in terms of some key indicators.

If you want to fast track, you can and you will start to notice changes. However, to create lasting change, you must commit to completing the full six-week transformation. Once you start, I promise you'll feel so good, more relaxed and happy with your life that you will continue this practice and stay in the zone.

Step Into Your Happiness Now

The urgency of writing this book has transformed into a mission. Discontent in the world is higher than usual, to say the least. At the time of this writing, we face a global pandemic and an economic crisis, with no idea of how the world will forever change. What is apparent to me, and the people and communities I work with is that underlying stress and emotions are now present within us each day. The ones we usually sweep under the rug so we can get on with our lives have become so much louder and more pronounced, that we're all forced to look inwards for solace. Our brains seem to be in constant reaction mode.

What better time to take a step back, retrain and R.E.W.I.R.E. our brains for greater peace, better health, and more happiness? Within the **R.E.W.I.R.E. System™**, you'll find the tools to cope with daily anxiety and worry, manage your stress, and find clarity no matter what's going on in the world. As you read through this book, do the practices, and shift your mindset, you'll cultivate that inner peace. You're also likely to find a sense of ease in all that you do, as well as many more opportunities to bring purpose and satisfaction to your life.

The very fact that you picked up this book means you're ready for change. You're ready to step into a happier, more powerful version of yourself. As a coach and educator, it's my privilege to help you live to your fullest potential. Are you ready? Let's do this!

It's Not You—Happiness is Hard to Find

We want happiness, less stress, more freedom, quality time with friends and family, no financial worries, a better quality of life. We are socialized to believe that if we achieve certain life goals—a better car, bigger house, better job, more pay, get married, have children—that they will equate to happiness. But do they? Don't get me wrong, we feel a great sense of pride, joy, fulfillment, a great sense of accomplishment with each of these milestones, but they never quite fill our cup. Why is that?

With the fulfillment of each of these goals, we have more to do, more financial obligations, more stress, and less time and inclination to look after our mental, emotional and physical health. Achieving these goals has the double-edged sword of more responsibility and less freedom. We seem to find moments of joy throughout the day, but our days are also permeated with worry and even anxiety. While we long for hope, peace, calm and happiness, most of us experience an undercurrent of stress instead.

This reminds me of one of my clients. When I first met Will, he appeared to have an idyllic life and seemed full of excitement and vitality.

The picture of good health and happiness, I met Will at a social event about eight years ago. In his 50s, he had a wonderful family and a successful business, which he stepped away from each winter to cruise around the Caribbean. Like I said, idyllic. But a few months after we met he called and asked to meet me for coffee.

When we did, I was surprised to see a completely different person in front of me. Tired, worn out and depressed, he explained that many areas of his life were unraveling and he needed my help. He wanted to hire me as a performance and mindset coach. I have worked with dozens of global executives and coached individuals and industry leaders on how to unlock what they need in order to be happier, healthier and thrive in both their personal and professional lives.

I knew immediately that I could help. The first part of working with a client usually entails understanding where they are now and where they want to be. The second part is where I help them uncover their unique nature so they can understand what they truly need in order to feel their very best. Next, I help them bridge the gap between where they are now and the life they want to live. Lastly, we develop a plan together to help them create this deeper sense of happiness and wellbeing so that they can live a life that truly has them thriving!

Goal Achievement vs. Happiness

So why do we strive for goal achievement thinking it will pave our way to happiness? Because that's what we're taught to do. And we try so hard, don't we? To dream of and achieve those goals? To be the best we can be? To be happier? Whether it's little things like trying to lose ten pounds and get in better shape or trying to be a better parent, person, employee, boss or friend. We try so hard to find that secret place where we can finally feel relaxed, yet accomplished. Feel like we can have everything we need, but with a sense of ease. Yet, we never quite get there. It's always just beyond reach. There's always one more thing to do.

I say secret because we all silently feel like we are the only ones getting it wrong. The majority of people in my coaching practice confess to me that they quietly feel as though they're failing. Like they are actors in a play, acting as though life comes easily, as though they know what they're doing and how to be happy and successful. In truth, most of us look around us and see people who seem to have it all together, but feel like they are the only ones that don't. News flash—most people don't have it all together. Just like us, they're pretenders too.

After our initial few sessions, we got to Will's true story. He had spent years cultivating a life that he thought would make him happy. Then a few small changes in his circumstances occurred and he began to spiral. Life happens. To all of us. Sometimes, life events occur in order to bring attention to the fact that what we were building and calling happiness isn't actually what truly makes us happy. Without a deep understanding and a sense of awareness of what we really need, we have no way of bridging our own gap. Like Will, we have no clear idea about what changes we need to make in order to reset. Will highlighted all of the life goals he chased and had no problem checking off those he accomplished and even surpassed. From the outside, Will had a quality of life most would envy. So what was missing?

When I tried to ask Will the deeper questions around what he needed, I realized he had been checking boxes his whole life. He achieved, but never took the time to discover or even think about what really made him happy. We are socialized to do and achieve—always with an eye on the future. Our culture puts that pressure on us first. Then we put it on ourselves. So is it any wonder that we mistake achievement for happiness? This is the root of what caused Will to be unhappy.

Will had accomplished everything he wanted. He'd been happily married for over twenty years, had two beautiful kids, a highly profitable business, a home in the country and the freedom to step away from his business and travel. By all rights, we would all be happy to have this life. Yet, there were some things causing changes in his life. Now, for anyone truly happy, you just learn to course correct a bit and find your stride again. I couldn't quite understand why a couple of life changes would cause him to unravel. It was clear that there was something deeper going on. He felt despondent and disconnected and felt shame around why he wasn't happier.

What Is Happiness Anyway?

Many feel happiness is this elusive state of being. We seem to find it in fleeting moments where we can laugh, enjoy quality time with loved ones, feel some relief from daily stress, relax, are more focused or maybe just get a good night's sleep. In other words, we can find happiness in moments where we find an overall sense of wellbeing. Happiness often shows up alongside feelings of fulfillment, contentment, peace, serenity, and true joy. And it's often accompanied by reduced stress levels, improved sleep, and fewer worries.

Will found he was happiest at his country home, or when he was able to travel, step away from his business, and spend time with his kids. Apart from that, when he was back in the city, it felt like a grind. His momentary sense of peace and relief vanished and he'd return to a state of melancholy. The challenge for most of us is to find a sustainable way to keep our sense of happiness consistent throughout the day, let alone from one day to the next. Some wonder if this kind of consistency is even possible. It is. Because while sustained happiness can't and won't be found in achieving outward goals, it can be cultivated by turning our efforts inward.

Our Internal Compass

Our emotions and feelings serve a purpose and we ignore them at our own peril. They are our internal compass that tells us how we're doing. They let us know if we're aligned, who we truly are and what makes us happy.

Most people think of emotions as good or bad. Good emotions being—joy, pride, excitement, and love, among others.. Bad emotions being—anger, sadness, fear, hurt, guilt, shame and grief. But what they really are—all of them—is a gauge, an indication to us when we are living according to our unique needs and personality, and when we are not.

When we are not, we are often in a state of uneasiness. We can't even describe why because we don't like to bring negative emotions into our consciousness. After all, negative emotions are usually signaling that something needs to change and human beings tend to resist change. So what happens when those negative emotions show up? We bury them. Deep. However, just because something is buried, doesn't mean it goes away. Eventually, those buried emotions make themselves known in our bodies. First, as a nagging tension, then discomfort, then anxiety, then pain, depression and sometimes, disease. Look at that word again—dis-ease.

So, do we give the issue our attention then? Nope. We avoid the pain by numbing ourselves further with various distractions—food, drugs, alcohol, shopping, sports, work, and the list goes on. While at first, our numbing activity of choice can seem fun, it can quickly devolve into an unhealthy pattern. We put on a façade and play a role of doing our best, doing what's expected of us—hoping it will make us happy and bring us stability. But it's not always easy to wake up each day feeling rested, energized and able to conquer the day ahead. Oftentimes, we feel tired, stressed, and worried about whether we can get to it all.

This is why I say that focusing on goal achievement rather than happiness has led us astray. Add to that, the fact we have no idea how to process our true feelings in any given moment and we've got a broken emotional compass. So when life events occur, as they will, we get derailed and have a hard time figuring out how to find our way and bounce back. More than that, we realize we aren't even sure where happiness is, so how could we possibly navigate back to it?

This is where Will found himself. Several years before I met him, he finalized a divorce, sold the country home that he loved, and took more time to travel. While he told himself he had accepted these changes, he didn't understand that these life events left an imprint. Sure, his divorce was amicable and he had a wonderful relationship with his children, but there was unprocessed grief from the divorce. Yes, his business was doing well and he could step away and enjoy some freedom, but he lacked a sense of purpose, experienced a loss of being needed and feeling more connected to his team, and the loss of the love of leadership. But his brain concocted a story, *this is what I've been working towards. I should be happy. Anyone in my position would be happy.*

We are so wired to avoid negative thoughts that oftentimes, we don't even know when we are unhappy until it hits us more seriously. Will confessed finally that he thinks he may even be depressed. Our brains are actually wired for survival, rather than to thrive and be happy. Being wired for survival worked when we lived in caves and had to run from imminent danger. In those days, our brains signaled our bodies to return back to our calmer state once we were out of danger.

What does survival feel like in our world? Let's just take an ordinary example. You wake up tired, instead of rested. You get ready to go to work, keep busy, manage the stresses of the day, wondering if you will have enough time and energy to get through it all. We run on auto-pilot most of the day, managing events and thwarting issues as they arise.

When we get home, we have strategies to decompress. Some work out, some socialize, some drink. Some drink a lot, just to turn off the brain and numb the anxiety or wash off the day. After an evening of doing whatever it is we do, we climb back into bed knowing we have to do it all again tomorrow. It's like there is an undercurrent of stress and anxiety with us every day and when we hear it, we automatically turn down the volume and press on. This is a stress response.

Until the day a life event occurs and we don't know how to process our feelings. All of those suppressed emotions become overwhelming and need to express themselves in some way. They can show up in a myriad of ways—pain and inflammation in the body, high blood pressure, heart disease, anxiety disorders, stress-related illness, job loss, relationships ending and so much more. At that moment, we have to pay attention. Finding happiness becomes necessary for our survival.

And So We Must Rewire

Over time, we've strengthened our stress response and weakened our bodies' natural ability to remain calm and happy. Unlike our ancestors, we don't have to suddenly flee from the very real threat of a predator chasing us. Luckily, we live in a more manageable world and aren't under real and constant threat. We can learn to rewire our brains to prioritize our happiness without jeopardizing our survival. In fact, there's significant evidence to suggest that happiness will ensure a healthier, longer life.[3]

With the right set of tools, all it takes is six weeks for the brain to show signs of lasting change. I developed this six-week program, so you can learn about what unique things make you happy. In these six weeks, you'll get to develop a personal plan, with me as your coach, to ensure you understand what really makes you feel alive. Together, we will move away from survival and move towards happiness through a series of exercises to reset and rewire your brain back to calm.

That's what Will and I did. His happiness is no longer tied to a story about his achievements. He no longer lives in the city, grinding away at his business, waiting for the winters in the Caribbean, wondering why he's not happy. Instead, he discovered he is most at peace in the country. He purchased a huge property on a lake in Muskoka, Ontario. He even moved his offices outside of the city so he could live full-time surrounded by nature. He found a lovely woman, who loves the country as much as he does and they are happily married. He is very clear on the things that make him happy and what causes him to be uneasy. And he knows how to reset and get back to happiness because his internal compass works again. Just like Will, you will be able to enjoy the same six-week program and rewire your brain for greater happiness.

PART II:

THE 6 WEEK TO R.E.W.I.R.E. SYSTEM™

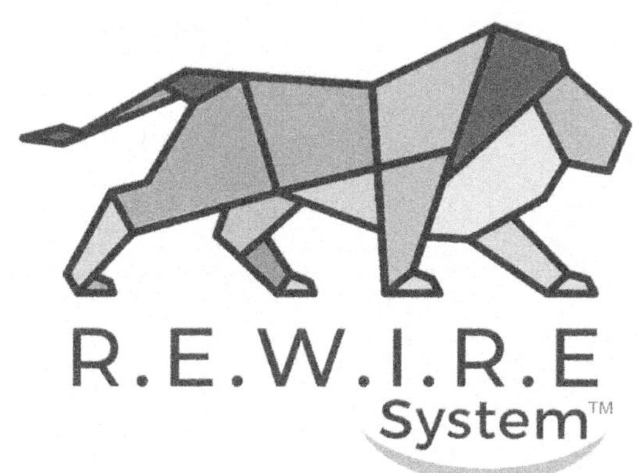

Week 1:
R = RELAX AND QUIET THE MIND

"Nowhere can you find a quieter or more untroubled retreat than in your own soul."

—**Marcus Aurelius,** Roman Emperor (161-180), Stoic philosopher

This week, using mindfulness and meditation, we will rewire our brain to restore our more natural, calm state. We will also look at the underlying beliefs that are keeping us in a state of stress. This week is about developing self-awareness, *allowing* ourselves to spend more time in a state of relaxation and then *consciously choosing* to do so.

Our brain is wired to protect us, flee from fear and danger, and keep us safe. This predisposition exists because, back in the day, our ancestors had to flee from real physical danger—think tigers in the bushes! This sudden jolt of life-threatening stress triggers something called our fight-or-flight response and acts like a gas pedal. Adrenaline floods the body so we can go into overdrive and quickly find safety. In the past, once the danger disappeared, and we knew we were okay, our brains would signal the body to return to our calm, natural state of being called rest-and-digest.

These days, life is busy and doesn't seem to slow down. With today's stresses, we are constantly being triggered as though we are always in fight-or-flight mode. Without realizing it, we've heightened our ability to become stressed because daily life these days often triggers our fight-or-flight response. Over time, we've weakened our body's natural ability to stay calm.

Just like a weight routine at the gym, repeated over the years, we can strengthen and build our emotional muscles over time or weaken them. Training our brain to be calm increases our ability to stay in rest-and-digest mode, shortening the time needed to return to this relaxed state when stressful events occur. Practicing meditation is one of the easiest ways to train your brain for greater calm.

A good example of the fight-or-flight lifestyle comes from one of my clients, a CEO of a major tech firm. When I asked him about his morning routine, he told me he would wake up and put on all the news networks in literally every room of his home. He felt he was gearing up for battle, and knowing everything that was going on in the world was a kind of pre-war ritual. After he had his shower, he walked from his bathroom to the kitchen to get coffee and he'd be informed no matter where he roamed in the house.

"It's like I'm putting on my armor for the day," he said.

"Have you ever just considered starting the day off calmly? You know, if you do that, it's not going to take away your edge," I said.

That's the fear. That by taking the time to be quiet, tune in, and find peace, people will somehow lose something in the process. Instead of understanding that the process of relaxing and quieting the mind isn't about losing something but actually adding to life. By finding more peace people are automatically *more productive.*

Practice Self-Awareness

What is self-awareness? It's the conscious understanding of one's own character, motives, feelings and desires. It's the deep knowledge of ourselves—what works for us and what doesn't. It's knowing ourselves, and then being true to ourselves.

Many of us go through life working and socializing to avoid being alone. As I touched on earlier, it's so important to start to tap into an understanding of ourselves so that we can enjoy the still moments and find peace and comfort in our own company. This will give you enormous inner strength if you can master this self-knowledge in the right way.

So how does one develop healthy self-awareness?

Start by just taking notice of how you feel in every moment. Start to notice how people and situations make you feel. Do they give you energy or take it from you? Do you feel calm, relaxed, and happy around them? Does it feel good or bad? Does it serve you and bring meaning to your life?

After asking these questions, you'll start to notice things more clearly. People and situations will feel lighter or heavier. You'll feel more interested in engaging in things that feel good to you. In a short time, you'll have less interest in the things that don't feel good.

Soon, you'll choose not to engage in situations where you feel drained of energy. After some time, you'll notice you feel happier and more energized than before. And it's not really even because you made a massive shift. You're simply taking the time to notice things about yourself.

Once you learn to develop some self-awareness, things will easily shift for you. You will naturally feel more inclined to spend time doing things that make you feel good. To be clear, we can engage in many things that feel good in the moment, which we might regret the next morning. I'm talking more about the activities that give you a deeper sense of contentment, a deeper sense of excitement or peace as opposed to fulfilling whims or fantasies.

On the other hand, if you're aware of what is good for you versus what isn't, and you are still choosing to engage, then there is more work to be done as to why you are continuing to perpetuate this pattern. If you can get to a point where you choose only what feels good wherever possible, you will feel an enormous sense of relief. Life will begin to feel lighter, easier and so will you. Feelings of overwhelm and unease will fade. At the same time, you're making more positive choices for your life, you are retraining your brain to feel good and this leads to feeling good much more often.

Meditation

While you may be uncomfortable with the concept at first, it can bring about enormous health benefits and happiness. Some of the most successful people in the world, including Tony Robbins, Katy Perry, Sir Paul McCartney, Jerry Seinfeld and the late Steve Jobs, have begun their days with the practice of meditation so they can focus on what's important to them.

> *"It's a heightened state of being that lets whatever you're doing be your best life, from moment to astonishing moment. The outside world is constantly trying to convince you you're not enough. But you don't have to take the bait. Meditation helps you resist."*
>
> —Oprah Winfrey, Media Executive, Television Producer, and Philanthropist

There is an overwhelming amount of research that has come out over the last 20 years that provides scientific proof of the benefits of meditation. If you absolutely do not want to be happy, don't do it!

Benefits of Meditation

- **Increased energy and productivity.**
- **Boosts your immunity and decreases the risk of disease.** A team of doctors at the Massachusetts General Hospital asked patients suffering from high blood pressure to try a meditation-

based relaxation program for three months. These were patients whose blood pressure had not been well controlled with medication. After meditating regularly for 3 months, 40 of the 60 patients showed significant drops in blood pressure levels and were able to reduce some of their medication.[4]

- **Reduces stress and anxiety.** Meditation can also lower the levels of cortisol—the stress hormone which keeps you in fight-or-flight. Reducing levels of cortisol allows for more relaxation and lets the body be in its calmer state.

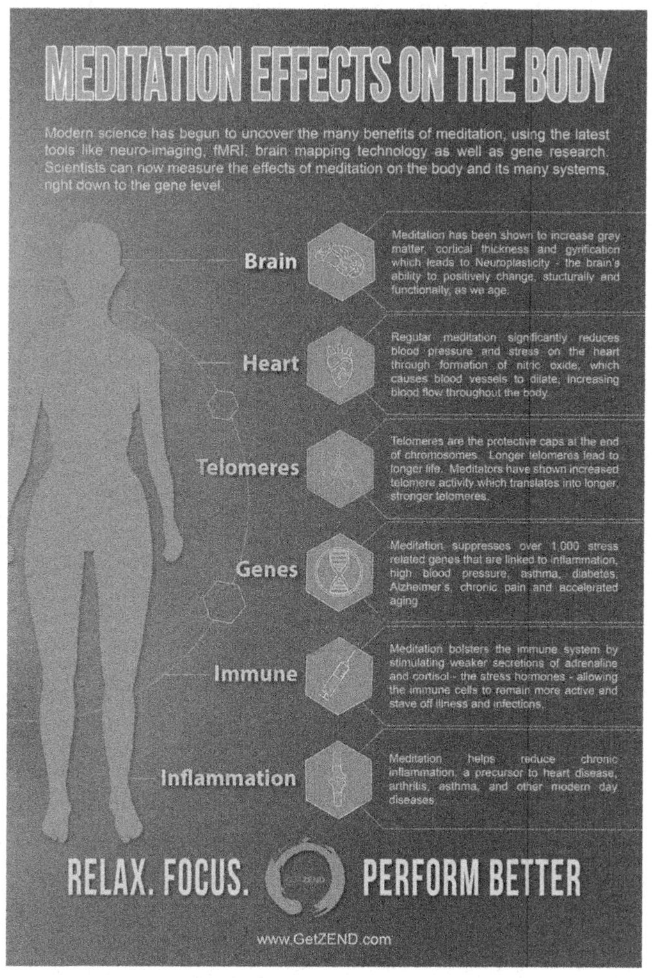

- **Silent meditation, walking meditation or repeating a mantra**—such as a word or phrase—during meditation can also have a calming effect, and by concentrating on your mantra, you're able to shift your focus away from distracting and worrying thoughts.
- **Transcendental meditation has a similar effect.** With Transcendental Meditation, it's usually practiced for 20 minutes per day, twice per day, and you silently repeat a word or sound to keep yourself focused. "As a result, you're able to reach a state of complete stillness and stability",[5] says David Foley, founder of Unify Cosmos, a meditation center in Oklahoma. A 2019 study showed a reduction in psychological distress among teachers and support staff who participated in a transcendental meditation program.[6] Researchers used stress scales before and after the program to measure the participants' levels of burnout, depression, and stress. After receiving a seven-step transcendental meditation course, participants reported lower levels of stress and burnout than before learning the techniques.
- **Increases your overall sense of well-being.** It helps develop positive social connections, improves your mood and increases emotional intelligence. Mindfulness meditation helps train your mind to focus on the present, making you less likely to ruminate on worrying thoughts that can fuel stress, anxiety and depression. A 2014 research analysis published in JAMA Internal Medicine found that mindful meditation can help ease anxiety and depression, and could be part of a comprehensive mental health treatment plan.[7] Studies have found that mindfulness-based stress reduction programs can help those with anxiety calm their minds and reduce common symptoms of depression, including trouble sleeping, loss of appetite and low mood.
- **Reduces worry and impulsivity.** Improves resilience against pain and adversity and reduces fear and loneliness.
- **Enhances self-esteem and self-acceptance**. Mindfulness meditation encourages you to slow down, allows for deeper

self-reflection, and can help you discover and focus on positive attributes about yourself. This increases optimism, self-awareness and relaxation.

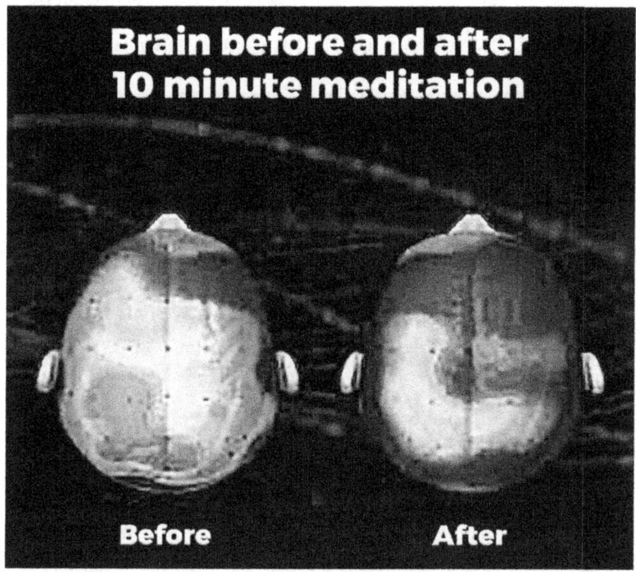

"According to researchers at Stanford University, mindfulness meditation can especially help those with social anxiety. In a 2009 study published in the Journal of Cognitive Psychotherapy, 14 participants with social anxiety disorder participated in two months of meditation training and reported decreased anxiety and improved self-esteem after completing the program."[8]

- **Increases focus, creativity and productivity.** Mindfulness[9] meditation helps you focus on the present, which can improve your concentration on other tasks in daily life. A 2011 study from Harvard Medical School[10] examined the effects of mindfulness meditation on the brain and found a connection between mindfulness and processing new information. The brains of 17 people before and after participating in an eight-week meditation program. Brain scans showed an increase in gray matter in the parts of the brain responsible for learning, memory, and emotional regulation. In Lazar et al.'s (2005) study, people who meditated a mere 40 minutes a day showed that they had thicker cortical walls than non-meditators. "... There were signs that their brains were aging at a slower rate. Cortical thickness is also associated with decision making, attention and memory."[11]

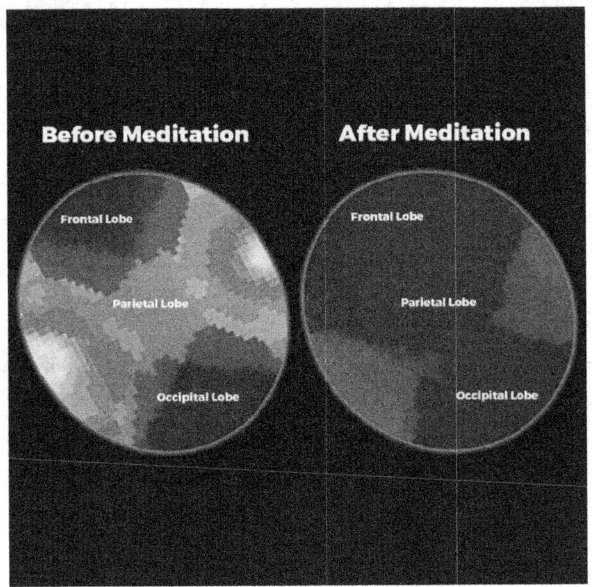

TOOL # 1:
Practice Mindfulness

"The quality or state of being conscious or aware of something. It's a mental state achieved by focusing one's awareness on the present moment, while calmly acknowledging and accepting one's feelings, thoughts, and bodily sensations, used as a therapeutic technique."

—The Oxford dictionary definition of *mindfulness*

There has been much speculation about mindfulness. Some confuse it with meditation as though they are the same—they're not. Learning how to practice mindfulness feels a bit like time is slowing down, giving you time to just breathe, pause, and observe yourself. Rather than a constant jog on the hamster wheel, we get to step down off of it, practice the pause (more on this useful tool later), and just be aware of how we respond.

The simple act of witnessing allows us to disengage from the cognitive functions that have us over-analyzing or worrying, and enables us to focus our attention on just being present with our breath and the sensations in our body, for example. Mindfulness can be practiced in a variety of ways—walking meditations, yoga, tai chi and qigong, or even exercise—anything that connects the mind with the body and breathwork. But most of the research comes from mindfulness meditation—self-regulation practices that focus on training attention and awareness in order to bring mental processes under increased voluntary control (versus running on auto-pilot). Meditation practice fosters healthier mental well-being and the development of specific capacities such as calm, clarity and concentration.[12]

In an article on the benefits of mindfulness, published in the journal for the American Psychological Association[13] researchers found that mindfulness meditation promotes metacognitive awareness, decreases the tendency for rumination and enhances attentional capacities through gains in working memory. These cognitive gains also contribute to better emotional regulation.

"Mindfulness helps increase self-awareness by increasing the ability to examine one's thoughts and feelings without judgment, which ends up improving self-esteem." [14]

— **Brian Wind, Ph.D.,** Chief Clinical Officer at JourneyPure

Benefits of Mindfulness

- **Reduced rumination.** If you're like me and highly analytical, eliminating rumination is extremely helpful in quieting the mind. In one study[15] Chambers et al. asked 20 novice meditators to take part in a 10-day intensive mindfulness meditation retreat. After the retreat, the meditation group had significantly higher self-reported mindfulness and showed a decrease in negative affect (or emotions and expression) compared with a control group. They also experienced fewer depressive symptoms and less rumination. In addition, the meditators had significantly improved working memory capacity and were better able to sustain attention compared to the control group.
- **Stress reduction.** In 2010, Hoffman et al. conducted a meta-analysis of 39 studies that explored the use of mindfulness-based stress reduction and mindfulness-based cognitive therapy.[16] Researchers concluded that mindfulness meditation increases positive affect and decreases anxiety and negative affect. In one study, participants randomly assigned to an eight-week mindfulness-based stress reduction group were compared with controls on self-reported measures of depression, anxiety and psychopathology, and on neural reactivity as measured by fMRI after watching sad films.[17] Researchers found that the participants who experienced mindfulness-based stress reduction had significantly less anxiety, depression and somatic distress compared with the control group. Also, the fMRI data indicated that the mindfulness group had less neural reactivity when they were exposed to the films than the control group, and they

displayed distinctly different neural responses while watching the films than they did before their mindfulness training. This suggests that mindfulness meditation shifts our ability to use emotional regulation in a way that enables us to experience emotion selectively (In other words, we have more choice over how we feel and how we react, we are not our emotions), and that the emotions experienced may be processed differently in the brain.[18]

- **Boosts to working memory.** A 2010 study[19] by Jha et al., documented the benefits of mindfulness meditation among a military group who participated in an eight-week mindfulness training, a non-meditating military group and a group of non-meditating civilians. Both military groups were in a highly stressful period before deployment. Of the three groups, the meditating military group showed working memory capacity increased with meditation practice. Again, meditation practice showed an increase in self-reported positive affect and a reduction in self-reported negative affect.
- **Focus.** A study examined how mindfulness meditation affected participants' ability to focus attention and suppress distracting information. They found that the meditation group had significantly better performance on all measures of attention and had higher self-reported mindfulness.[20]
- **Less emotional reactivity.** In a study of people who had anywhere from one month to 29 years of mindfulness meditation practice, researchers found that mindfulness meditation practice enabled people to disengage from emotionally upsetting pictures and enabled them to focus better on a cognitive task as compared with people who saw the pictures but did not meditate.[21]
- **More cognitive flexibility.** Another line of research suggests that in addition to helping people become less reactive, mindfulness meditation may also give them greater cognitive flexibility. One study found that people who practice mindfulness meditation appear to develop the skill of self-observation, which

neurologically disengages the automatic pathways that were created by prior learning and enables present-moment input to be integrated in a new way.[22] This begins to disconnect us from our old neural pathways, our old ways of thinking and feeling and allows us space for new wiring in the brain. Meditation also activates the brain region associated with more adaptive responses to stressful or negative situations.[23] Activation of this region corresponds with faster recovery to baseline after being negatively provoked.[24] And so begins our training away from survival strategies and back to calm, giving us back control and more choice over how we respond to the world.

- **Relationship satisfaction.** Several studies have found that a person's ability to be mindful assists with the ability to respond well to relationship stress and in improving communication around emotions to a partner. Empirical evidence suggests that mindfulness protects against the emotionally stressful effects of relationship conflict,[25] is positively associated with the ability to express oneself in various social situations[26] and predicts relationship satisfaction.[27] If mindfulness has us more aware, less stressed, better able to regulate emotions and improves our ability to maintain healthy relationships, sign me up!

If that's not enough to convince you, mindfulness has also been shown to enhance self-insight, morality, intuition and fear modulation. Evidence also suggests mindfulness meditation has numerous health benefits, including increased immune functioning[28] [29], improvement of well-being[30] and reduction in psychological distress.[31] [32] In addition, mindfulness meditation practice appears to increase information processing speed[33], as well as decrease task effort and having thoughts that are unrelated to the task at hand.[34]

Mindfulness is a no-brainer—tasks get easier, we become more focused and peaceful; have less stress, worry, anxiety and depression; a reduced response to fear; better immune function; and healthier relationships. Yes, please!

MEDITATION EFFECTS ON THE BRAIN

MRI scans have shown that meditation increases gyrification, or cortical folding, which allows the brain to process information faster.

Meditation increases whole brain function by synchronizing the left and right hemisphere of the brain. It increases balance and amplitude in alpha, theta and delta brainwave frequencies.

PRODUCTIVITY

Brain Function

Meditation increases dopamine and serotonin - the "feel good hormones" - by stimulating regions of the brain associated with happiness and positivity.

Meditation improves focus by increasing cortical thickness in regions of the brain responsible for attention.

Focus

Mood

Stress Reduction

Cognition

Meditation reduces stress and anxiety by decreasing adrenaline and cortisol - the stress hormones - allowing your body to stay in a deeper state of relaxation, where your breathing, pulse rate, blood pressure and metabolism are in the healthier zones.

Meditation improves cognitive function, mindfulness and the ability to maintain focus. It increases gray matter, brain volume and cerebral blood flow.

RELAX. FOCUS. PERFORM BETTER

GETZEND

www.GetZEND.com

"Mindfulness is a **moment-to-moment, non-judgmental awareness,** *cultivated by paying attention in a specific way, that is, in the present moment, and as* **non-reactively,** *as* **nonjudgmentally,** *and as* **open-heartedly** *as possible."*

—**Jon Kabat-Zinn,** an American professor emeritus of medicine and the creator of the Stress Reduction Clinic and the Center for Mindfulness in Medicine, Health Care, and Society at the University of Massachusetts Medical School.

TOOL # 2:

Identify Your Limiting Core Beliefs & Develop Self Awareness

It has become very clear to me, through my research and experience coaching hundreds of clients, that we have all suffered childhood trauma, adolescent challenges and painful experiences that have shaped who we are and how we interact with the world. The suffering we experience forces us to either grow and evolve or we end up repeating the old patterns until we heal.

If we choose not to heal or don't realize we need to be healed, we will continually get triggered and presented with an opportunity to heal. These opportunities present themselves as tricky situations, people that hurt or disappoint us, relationship issues, health issues, and failed attempts at happiness and prosperity.

As we go through this journey called life, we are meant to evolve in order to find greater peace, better health, more balance, more joy, gratitude and to find meaning. The early trauma that occurs usually leaves us with a set of limiting core beliefs. This is where most of our self-doubt comes from, and forms our trust or lack of trust in relationships—like fear of abandonment, and feelings of not being worthy.

The 5 Main Limiting Core Beliefs

In my experience working with hundreds of clients I've discovered there are Five Main Limiting Core Beliefs that are common to most people:

- I'm Not Loved (or I'm Unworthy of Being Loved)
- I'm Undeserving of Wealth or Success or a Life I Love
- I'm Alone (or Unsupported)
- I'm Not Safe (or not Protected)
- I'm Not (Good) Enough

I'm Alone (or Unsupported)

There may be variations to these five. For example, a client named Richard was a CEO of a global company, extremely hard-working, and successful by anyone's standard. He didn't have any issues believing in himself and knew from a very young age that he would always do very well in business and run a large company. And he did.

His personal life, however, was another matter. He had a deep and raw belief that he was unworthy of love and that he was alone, so he needed validation from everyone he met. He needed to be the center of attention so much that he had no boundaries and his relationships suffered. He desperately wanted love and partnership but was not capable of being in a healthy, wholehearted relationship. So he sabotaged relationships with any potential partner. Afraid of being alone and afraid that he wasn't loveable, he made sure to always surround himself with people, regardless of whether or not they were people of quality, which left no space to confront the parts of him that needed healing.

The subconscious limiting beliefs here—I'm alone and I'm not loveable. He had such a fear of abandonment that he would routinely cause trauma to the relationship, creating issues, proving that he actually was unloveable. Since he didn't feel safe to love anyone, he'd continually do enough damage to the relationship that the person he loved, the one person he wished would love him back, would eventually leave.

What did you hear growing up?

What are some of the common beliefs held by you, or family or friends that may be impacting you at a subconscious level and affecting your progress? For example, what are your beliefs around finances, money and career?

"Money doesn't grow on trees"
"Struggle is the meaning of life"
"Anything worth having takes hard work"
"Money is the root of all evil"
"All you need is enough to survive"

Really take time to think about each of these and note how they may have shaped your core beliefs.

A note about trauma

Now, let's go back to the conversation about how we evolved to be good at survival. When trauma occurs, we create meaning and our subconscious mind tells a story as to WHY the trauma is happening. In Richard's case, when his mother used to give him tough love and he was teased by his siblings, he told himself that he was alone in the world and no one really loved him and his survival strategy became the story of "I don't need anyone."

These are all stories meant to protect us, keep us safe, help us survive, and help us stay alive. These strategies or patterns of behavior then get coupled with the emotions that show up in those moments, like sadness or fear, and they become physically anchored within us and stored as memories that are locked together. Those negative emotions, the limiting belief(s) and the strategy (or pattern of behavior) all get bundled together and recorded in our emotional and mental bodies.

To simplify our example, that negative emotion of sadness and the limiting belief *I'm not loved* get attached to each other. Our protective strategy *I don't need anyone* then gets coupled with *sadness* and the limiting belief. Here's how it would play out. The next time sadness shows up, that whole bundle of stuff gets triggered—when I feel sad and unloved, I need to protect myself, I'll push the person away and strike out so they know who's in charge and so that I don't get hurt again.

The next time anything happens that reminds us of the original trauma, we get triggered and that same pattern, that same strategy plays out as though we are on auto-pilot. We are not in control, we are not driving the car at that moment. We are just a passenger and our pattern takes the driver's seat. We have to wait until the pattern plays out and the car comes to a stop before we can think clearly again. Just pause and process that for a moment...see how it plays out in your life when this happens. And it happens to us all.

Think of how much hurt and pain we can save ourselves if we were just willing to go back and look at which of these five limiting core beliefs are within us? Once identified, we would finally be able to heal and stop ourselves from being triggered and repeating destructive patterns over and over again. Imagine the freedom that comes from seeing a situation unfolding and knowing in that split second where you would normally react, it's as if time slowed down, and you can actually make a different choice of how to respond?

This is the healing that takes place and the trauma that gets cleared in the mental and emotional bodies so that we can have more volitional choice about how we interact with the world. *It gives us back our power to choose* how we respond. Once this healing begins and the awareness is developed, *you can't unsee it.* It may show up in another form later, but you'll recognize it, and catch yourself and you'll get to choose. And that's powerful.

Write it down

Look at these five limiting core beliefs and develop some awareness around how they impact your life, your beliefs, your relationships, your choices, your finances and how you spend your time. At the end of the book, you will have a chance to go through this in more detail as a series of exercises. For now, just grab a notebook or journal and a pen and start writing each one down and notice how that belief might play out in your life. Notice who and what events in your life trigger you. Notice that it's not just the person doing the triggering but the YOU that's being triggered because there is still a part of you that needs healing.

Lastly, please just learn to observe yourself without judgment. Allow for some space between you—the person that's healing—and you the observer. There is no right or wrong. These are the human experiences that connect us all and that we all have in common. The details of your life story may be different, but we have all felt these limiting beliefs at some point in our lives, in some way. With a little patience and the willingness to do the work, we can all begin to heal and find the peace we seek. It just takes a small shift to recognize the belief, name it, and create some separation so we can witness, take a step back and let healing begin.

TOOL # 3: Meditation—Retrain Your State Of Calm

Over the past few decades, the benefits of regular meditation have been well proven.[35] As we stated earlier, benefits include decreased stress, improved focus, boosted immunity, lower blood pressure, and reduced symptoms of anxiety and depression, just to name a few. While there are different types of meditation, they can all offer a similar set of proven benefits for mental and physical health. In terms of emotional well-being, meditation lessens worry and impulsivity, reduces fear and loneliness, enhances self-esteem and self-acceptance, improves resilience against pain and adversity, increases optimism, self-awareness and relaxation. Meditation helps develop positive social connections, improves your mood and increases emotional intelligence.

Neuroscience Research on Meditation

Neuroscientist Richard Davidson has shown that experienced meditators exhibit high levels of gamma wave activity compared to those that do not have a meditation practice. Gamma waves are able to link information from all parts of the brain, making it more coherent. Gamma waves have been said to be the "feeling of blessings" reported by experienced meditators such as nuns or monks. Gamma waves are associated with peak concentration and high levels of cognitive function—an ability that continues even after the meditation session has ended. This means you are more likely to not get stuck on a particular situation or stimulus, making it easier to regulate reactions and thoughts. Meditators are likely to have a more resilient brain.[36]

The trick with meditation is to find a way to practice that resonates with you. You can find a guided meditation online or you can sit in silence if that feels better for you. If you feel like you have trouble quieting your thoughts, don't resist them or make yourself wrong; just breathe through it. Allow your thoughts, observe them, then breathe and refocus on being still or focus on your goals. You can use an app like the one I've developed, called GetZENd—download at **www.getzend.com**—which incorporates many of the tools from neuroscience and the study of success to help you do this if you're new to meditation.

The GetZENd app has a guided coaching session called "Get Meditating," which will take you through specific cues of how to focus your breath, focus on the tension and release of tension in your body, or focus on various areas of your life. The app is designed to help you learn how to meditate and to continue that practice easily with a ready-to-use tool. It uses a blend of tools from neuroscience and hypnotherapy as well as sound wave technology to "tune in" to a desired relaxed brainwave. From there, you will be guided into a meditation where you can focus on different areas of your life, or you can choose to just listen to the brainwave music and enter a calmer state of mind.

For some people, meditation is more easily found when they connect with nature, like taking a walk on the beach or a walk in the woods. For others, they can sit peacefully in the sunshine or imagine themselves in their happy place, or a relaxed state. However, you choose to do it is fine. If you can sit in silence and quiet the mind, then you're ahead of the game. I was not one of the lucky ones. I needed some training to just be comfortable with it, let alone find a way to do it that worked for me. This led me to develop the GetZENd app so it was easier for you.

MEDITATION AND BRAINWAVES

Using neuro-imaging, fMRI, brain mapping technology and gene research, scientists can now measure the effects of meditation on the brain and brainwave patterns.

14-24hz Beta Waves

This is your "busy mind", also called the "monkey mind" which we all experience. Beta waves are characterized by chaotic, unbalanced thinking, typical of left brain dominance.

8-13hz Alpha Waves

The beginning of balanced brainwave activity. As you access more alpha waves in ordinary states of consciousness, the easier you can access deeper meditative states.

4-7.5hz Theta Waves

Balanced brainwave activity increases in Theta brainwaves. Theta waves correspond to the experience of intuitive, creative and "visionary" levels of experience.

0.5-4hz Delta Waves

Delta brainwaves correspond to the "beyond thought" or "beyond mind" experience of the subtlest levels of meditative awareness. This is the range in which meditators experience oneness with all things or the "universal consciousness".

RELAX. FOCUS.

PERFORM BETTER

www.GetZEND.com

Not into meditating, I can relate...I avoided it for decades

If I wrote it a letter, it would have sounded like this—

Hey Meditation,
Sigh... We've come full circle. I don't understand you, but you keep popping into my life to tell me you can help. Many are your greatest fans. Some find you strange and.... different. Some are confused by you because they think it may clash with their existing beliefs. But at this point, you have been highly recommended by literally every professional I respect, so, I think it's time I pay attention and give you a try. Even though I've been raised in a faith where meditation was taught, I just don't fully understand you or even know how to do it right. People that have not been raised with the concept of meditation seem to have embraced you and love having you in their life. And some shut down at the mere idea of you. So.... How do I welcome you and sit with you? People keep telling me we should get to know each other. I wasn't sure we'd get along. But I need something new in my life... so I'm just going to invite you in and see how we feel together.

Willing,
Zahra

I was lucky enough to be raised in a faith where we were taught not only to look after ourselves in this physical material world, but we also have to look after our spiritual health. I didn't really know what the spiritual part meant, though. I didn't really know how to meditate or if I was doing it right when I tried. Also, I didn't realize I was left-brained either. Things need to be logical and explained to me in a scientific way in order for me to understand and evaluate whether I'm interested in incorporating things into my life. I don't do anything by the seat of my pants, even meditation, apparently. When I tried to meditate I knew I felt good. And I didn't yet understand why. This sent me on a quest to understand the science behind the good feeling that meditation brings to those who practice.

Several months later, I had all this research behind me, and I'm back at work and meditating, living at a more relaxed pace. Yay me. I grew up a bit! But, back at home, though, my marriage was ending. That one hurt. But I accepted it almost as quickly as it startled me, and then took a bit of time to process it all.

The shock of my marriage ending after just a year was complicated by the grief I felt with this loss. Oh, the grief. That one is tough. It comes in waves. Just when you think you're up and standing, it knocks you down again. Then my amazing sister sent me the most perfect message on my birthday card.

It said, *"You can't stop the waves.... But you can learn to surf."* This has become my philosophy in life when things happen. And they do happen.

Well, after a few months of serious grieving, I decided it was enough. I needed to feel like myself again. So I thought, okay, I have all these tools at my disposal, let's get back to being strong, healthy and happy again. I didn't know where to start my road to recovery, so I just focused on the top five lessons I learned in my happiness research.

The search for happiness doesn't actually make us happy. In fact, it can do the opposite. Searching for happiness can serve to highlight all the things that are missing in our lives and, therefore, keeps us stuck in a scarcity mindset versus an abundance mindset. Instead of feeling blessed for all that we do have and welcoming new and wonderful things into our lives, we instead focus on all that's missing and so we create more of that. If you're missing love, then you keep reproducing a lack of love, either in your current relationship or in trying to develop a new one. Like a self-fulfilling prophecy—everything you believe to be true IS TRUE and we look for evidence to support it.

1. **Practicing gratitude shifts our awareness to what is already good in our lives and so begins to move us from scarcity to abundance.** We stretch out the amount of time spent feeling good versus time ruminating over feelings of lack. This can be

done in a myriad of ways—simply begin each day and end each day with a few things for which you are truly grateful, keep a gratitude journal, and take moments to remind yourself to be grateful throughout the day. The more you do this, the more you are training yourself to focus on the blessings instead of what is missing in your life.

2. **Developing Self Awareness or being mindful is a practice** where you are able to observe your own thoughts, without judgment.
3. **We need to develop emotional intelligence**, which is the ability to recognize our own emotions, the emotions of others and develop the ability to adjust our emotions as needed.
4. **Meditate.**
5. **Learning to be happy is a conscious choice every day,** like navigating a boat or plane, we have to constantly find flow or course correct to stay in the zone.

How I began meditating

I woke up a bit earlier to allow time to meditate in the morning and took a hot shower to wake up the body, as I always did before work. I poured myself a big mug of morning coffee and plopped down on my couch. After studying calming breathwork, I knew a few deep breaths with a slower exhale would get me into a more relaxed state of mind. Then I just focused on how I wanted to feel. I focused on three feelings—peaceful, calm, happy. I spent a few minutes on each one, really allowing me to *feel* that emotion and that state of being until my whole body felt calmer. After a few weeks, I started to really enjoy that time and it was the most blissful time of day. Meditation just started my day off right.

But, there's no wrong way to meditate. Start with even five minutes a day and slowly work your way up to twenty minutes if you can. It took me months to master my way up to twenty minutes. Now I'll sit for twenty or thirty minutes and I usually feel like only five minutes went by and I want more. It feels so good to be calm, relaxed, and be in that space of creation, that feeling of vacation, that I just want to stay there for longer. Some days I do. Some days I'll do whatever feels good, whether it's ten minutes or thirty. Taking time to master meditation is essential and a key component to retrain the brain for greater calm. When you're able to tap into how to meditate the right way for you, everything will feel easier.

> *"...meditation helps you stay in a clear-headed state so that when challenges come at you, you can deal with them like a ninja – in a calm, thoughtful way."*
>
> —**Ray Dalio,** American billionaire investor and philanthropist

> *"It feels like I'm home. Everyone gets used to the noise. Have you ever been in a room and you hear this humming sound and until it turns off, you didn't realize there was a noise? I had no idea how noisy everything was until I was still and quiet. I'm grateful to you for teaching me this because it's changed my life."*
>
> —**Ellen Degeneres,** Comedian and TV Host during her interview with Bob Roth, author and transcendental meditation teacher

> *"...your mind just slows down, and you see a tremendous expanse in the moment. You see so much more than you could see before. It's a discipline; you have to practice it."*
>
> —the late, great **Steve Jobs**, co-founder of Apple Inc.

Get ready to transform

Many of my friends have said to me, "It's amazing that you just think of something you'd like to do or have and then it appears in your life."

My meditation practice is the single most impactful thing I've ever done and it has transformed me and my life. It will transform your life too. Since I began the daily practice of meditation, I have found that I am much calmer, more at peace, focused, energized and happier than I've ever been in my life. When I meditate I have this feeling that everything will just come together easily and then it does.

When I meditate, I use that time to focus on my life or just sit quietly and find my peace. When I focus on what I'd like to create in my life, I imagine it's already happened. (More on why later). This shifts my mindset to one of creation and abundance. Rather than spending time worrying about what's not happening, I focus on all I've already got and imagine those new desires as having already manifested.

When I do, they show up in my life. Either a door opens or an opportunity pops up, or the very thing I've been wanting happens with ease. As we go through the workbook, we will break this down together into something YOU feel comfortable with. We will find exactly what will feel natural for you so that you can create a daily practice that leaves you feeling good.

Most people don't understand the power of their own thoughts and how they shape the world around us. Everything we think, do, feel and experience gets encoded in our brains and then produces our reality. We MUST master how to quiet the mind so that we can *choose* what we want to think, feel and do in order to be more in control of how we interact with the world around us.

Week 2:
E = ELIMINATE THE NOISE

"Our life is frittered away by detail. Simplify, simplify, simplify! I say, let your affairs be as two or three, and not a hundred or a thousand; instead of a million count half a dozen, and keep your accounts on your thumbnail."

—**Henry David Thoreau**, American Naturalist, poet, and philosopher

In Week 1: R = RELAX & Quiet the Mind, you learned the benefits of going inward to find some peace and retrain your body back to a calm state. This week, we'll take some time to look at the elements in our lives that keep us feeling stretched too thin, overly stressed, and we'll look at how we can reclaim our energy by making small changes in our life so that we can maintain the peace and quiet we've just learned to cultivate.

Too many of us have so many things in our lives demanding our time, money and energy. By taking an inventory of the things that require much of us and our time, we can then focus on the things we *must do* versus the things *we can do*, while still prioritizing our energy.

Let's Talk About Balance, Baby!

We've all heard that to live a good quality of life, we need to have "balance." But what does that actually mean? I could talk to any CEO or entrepreneur and they would balk at the notion of balance. Their version of balance is very different than it would be for others. Most high performers are so used to working long days and always thinking about business or innovation, that the idea of balance for them looks like waking up at 5 AM and not stopping until 11 PM, then doing it all over again. In the next section, we get into balance a bit more in terms of what each of us needs and what resonates for us.

For now, let's imagine that balance is about managing your energy. We have a finite amount of energy every week and it needs to be restored and replenished in order for us to start each new week refreshed. We'll talk about self-regulation, ego depletion and willpower in this section so you will get an understanding of the kinds of things that require your energy in a given week. Then, we'll talk about how to restore balance.

Why is restoring balance important? Once we uncover what takes our mental energy and hinders our ability to regulate our emotions and power to choose, wouldn't life get easier? Couldn't we take back some control over our life? Now the question becomes, can we neurohack a state where we are more in control and have more ability to choose what we need?

I'd say yes! When we're able to better manage our four-body system, we can create the ideal set of tools to boost our performance for a healthier, happier state of wellbeing.

Start With Self-Regulation

What is self-regulation really? Wikipedia defines it this way—"Self-regulation is the ability to monitor and manage your energy states, emotions, thoughts, and behaviors in ways that are acceptable and produce positive results such as well-being, loving relationships, and learning"

Well, who wouldn't want that? The ability to be more in control of ourselves? If I could command my body to not want dessert or to not get upset in certain situations or to have a deep restful sleep when I feel stressed, that would be awesome. I'm in!

Dr. Stuart Shanker, Founder of The MEHRIT Centre and the Self-Regulation Institute says, "Self-regulation is the ability to manage your own energy states, emotions, behaviors and attention, in ways that are socially acceptable and help achieve positive goals, such as maintaining good relationships, learning, and maintaining wellbeing."

If we take this view as an *intention* for wellbeing, then we can begin to make choices about how we spend our time in a way that is more aligned with *how we want to feel* in our lives.

Willpower & Ego Depletion

In their book, *Willpower: Rediscovering the Greatest Human Strength*, Baumeister and Tierney, talk about the links between ego depletion and willpower.

"While depleted persons didn't show any single telltale emotion, they did react more strongly to all kinds of things. A sad movie made them extra sad. Joyous pictures made them happier, and disturbing pictures made them more frightened and upset. Ice cold water felt more painful to them than it did to people who were not ego-depleted. Desires intensified along with feelings. After eating a cookie, people reported a stronger craving to eat another cookie – and they did in fact eat more cookies when given a chance. ...So if you'd like some advance warning of trouble, look not for a single symptom but rather for a change in the overall intensity of your feelings."[37]

In a very real way then, we can use willpower *as a gauge* for how well we are self-regulating. But we can't properly self-regulate when our ego is depleted. Wikipedia defines *Ego depletion* in this way—

"Ego depletion refers to the idea that self-control or willpower draws upon a limited pool of mental resources that can be used up. When the energy for mental activity is low, self-control is typically impaired, which would be considered a state of ego depletion. In particular, experiencing a state of ego depletion impairs the ability to control oneself later on. A depleting task requiring self-control can have a hindering effect on a subsequent self-control task, even if the tasks are seemingly unrelated. Self-control plays a valuable role in the functioning of the self on both individualistic and interpersonal levels. Ego depletion is, therefore, a critical topic in experimental psychology, specifically social psychology, because it is a mechanism that contributes to the understanding of the processes of human self-control."

Let's examine this idea in more simple terms. First, we are not referring to Ego here as in one's sense of self-esteem or self-importance. In the metaphysical sense, we are referring to Ego as a conscious thinking being and what drains or restores that being's energy.

There are certain tasks that take mental energy, such as work-related activities—decision making, operating a business, managing people and resources, strategic thinking and others. There is stress when you spend time with negative people (we'll talk about emotional contagion later), stretch your time after work, with family, and other social activities, without getting enough time for rest or self-care.

The most common sources of ego depletion are:

- Stress—Has us spend energy ruminating on multiple things at once
- Pain—It takes energy to negotiate with our brains to pay less attention to pain and focus instead on other activities
- Making decisions—Takes mental fuel as we weigh different options and use energy to problem solve
- Taking initiative or taking on a new challenge—We expend energy to process any anxiety or self-doubt that arises in order for us to move past the initial inertia to take that leap into action.

(Shout out to Emiliya Zhivotovskaya, Head of the Flourishing Center for this brilliant explanation.)

- Multi-tasking—Research has shown that the brain does not multitask. It can only focus on one task at a time. When we multitask, we are actually *task-switching* and that takes energy.
- Restraining Impulses—For example, if we are on a diet, we are practicing self-restraint, that resistance takes energy for some people.
- Sleep Deprivation—Sleep allows the body and brain to recharge, so getting less sleep than we need can keep our energy reserves low
- Low Blood Sugar—Creates stress on the body and the body needs to find a source of energy to regulate itself

This all makes such perfect sense! It's so much easier to resist temptation when we are relaxed! Think about the days when you're exhausted. You need so much more energy to accomplish your regular daily activities. Keeping an exercise routine or eating healthy doesn't feel as immediately rewarding as ordering that pizza or indulging in a glass of wine or that piece of chocolate—self-regulating is so much easier when you're feeling relaxed and energized!

Keys To Self-Regulation

Developing self-awareness or being mindful is a practice where you are able to observe your own thoughts, without judgment. Over time, you begin to see areas of yourself that need healing. We all have past hurt and trauma in different ways. Finding tools to heal from the past is helpful and try as we like to avoid it, is also necessary. Once you begin that healing, you also have the ability to catch yourself in old patterns of thinking.

You can witness how emotions cause patterns of behavior that no longer serve you. Once you become aware of the pattern, you can begin to process and release those emotions and ultimately, have a heightened awareness of yourself in different situations, of your inner dialogue, even. Eventually, you can then shift your thinking back to gratitude and abundance, back to self-love, back to compassion and a sense of peace.

Permission slip

Give yourself permission to be human. We all have old patterns of behavior that we can't seem to control. We all have emotional outbursts from time to time or coping mechanisms we wish we could better manage. We all have bad days among the good. It's okay to be emotional in those moments and then reset. We need to develop emotional intelligence (or EI), which is the ability to recognize our own emotions, the emotions of others and develop the ability to adjust our emotions as needed.

Less is more

As you can see, it's important for your well-being to stop engaging in activities and spending time with people that don't bring value to your life and drain you of your energy. It's important to learn how to edit your activities and relationships. My two favorite words are *Happy* and *Easy*. If I'm not feeling this way around the people I'm with, I either limit my time with them or choose to remove them from my life as much as possible, sometimes even completely.

But, this is not always possible. Clients often tell me the person in question is a family member or a high school friend or someone in their friendship circle. They may even feel guilty about the idea of limiting time with them. However, if you can allow yourself to put your happiness first, it's easier to minimize your time with these people or stick to subjects that are not contentious.

Even if setting a new boundary is challenging, it is possible to remove people from your social circle or avoid situations where you need to spend time with them. If you do need to spend time with them because your social circles and lives are intertwined, then keep the conversation light and breezy and don't engage in subjects that could bring about tension or drama.

Spending time with people that are anxious or who bring you down is not good for your health and wellbeing. If you're taking the time to find your way to happiness, then you have a right to choose what and with whom you spend your time. If an activity, social scene or person makes you feel drained, don't engage. Start to make a list of people and situations that have you feeling depleted or unhappy and edit them from your activities. When you learn precisely how to remove yourself from these scenarios and stay committed to yourself in all situations, you will find yourself feeling lighter, more creative, resourceful and relaxed. When you do, you will have more control over your mood, your energy and your emotions.

Learn How To Say *No!*

A great way to attain the goal of having control over your life involves learning how to draw healthy boundaries so you have enough energy to look after yourself and the people you love. You can't do everything for everyone all the time.

Life is busy. Many of us allow ourselves to be stretched too thin, trying to accomplish everything we think we need to in a day. Instead of trying to take everything on, prioritize your time with the activities you need to engage in with the people you need to see.

If you have trouble saying *no*, try this on—

"I would really love to...I just have other commitments at the moment."

Or find some other way of expressing that you are not available that feels authentic to you. Most of us hate saying *no* because we don't want to disappoint another person, so we say *yes* and overcommit ourselves. Things get much easier to manage when you're able to express your disappointment in not being able to do something by letting the other person know they're important to you, but that you are busy. People usually like hearing you would've liked to help, even if you cannot or will not. That way, you feel less like you've disappointed them, and your *no* was simply a conflict in schedules and nothing more.

Learning how to say *no* will make your days feel easier, bring opportunities into your life, and deepen your relationships. You also get to avoid the feeling of pending doom that begins the minute you utter the word *yes* when you know it would be nearly impossible to accomplish. When you prioritize your life, learn to say *no*, and draw healthy boundaries, people will understand that you can't put yourself under unnecessary pressure. You'll lighten your load and finally feel like you have enough time to get to the things you need and enjoy.

Don't Take It Personally

Sometimes, when you exercise your ability to say *no*, people won't understand. You may even have guilt projected onto you. There are other times when people will let you down in big and little ways. Learn forgiveness and compassion. Not because the offense was okay, but because people sometimes project their own negative emotions or fears onto us. Learn forgiveness, because, most likely, they are not meaning to hurt you.

People can only meet you as far as they've met themselves. If they've not healed past trauma, they will likely keep *projecting* it onto the people in their lives. If you can find a healthy level of detachment and practice knowing it's not about you, then you can forgive more easily. Forgive, because you deserve to be free of suffering. Forgiveness is particularly difficult for people who experienced unhappiness in their family upbringing or in their closest relationships. Sometimes we feel the most pain from our partner or family relationships because there is so much love and connection.

While we do have the power to hurt each other, most of us never mean to hurt another person. Usually, intentions are good. When things are done that are knowingly ill-intentioned, it likely happens when someone is not looking after their own needs, simply lacks self-awareness, or has some unhealed past trauma. The thing that was done to you is usually not about you—it's about the other person. If we can get to a space where we don't internalize the other person's actions—because *that place* is usually where the suffering comes from—then there is room for us to breathe.

'That place' is the one that has us asking the questions—

"Why?"

"Why am I not good enough?"

"What changed?"

"What's wrong with me that this happened?"

There's usually hurt attached here because we speak from a place of not being enough. And it doesn't matter who you are, 'that place' does not feel good. If you can, instead, speak from a place of understanding that the person who hurt you is on their own journey, then you understand that it's their process, and sometimes you are in the wake of their process.

Once you change your perspective into one of understanding, then there's space for healing to happen. Forgiveness doesn't excuse the actions of another person or make them right. It isn't reconciliation. But if the person who has committed an offense against you can take full responsibility and is able to acknowledge what happened (along with the who, where, when, how and why, etc.), then it opens up the opportunity for you to forgive and let go of the suffering. When you do, you can heal and make your way back to wholeness again.

Even if the person is not able to take responsibility, it's important that we forgive them and let go, so we can be free. Once the forgiveness has happened, you have a much clearer choice about whether or not to continue to have that person in your life and, if so, what form that relationship might take in the future, if at all. You can draw new boundaries and set new expectations for your future relationships, ensuring your needs are met.

When something does go wrong in a relationship, take time to forgive. Remember we are each on our own journey. We need to be patient with ourselves and with each other. Forgive, because we deserve to be free of the pain, the sadness, anger, and resentment. Forgive because you deserve to be happy.

You Already Have What You Need

Self-love and acceptance are the foundation for emotional maturity and what enables us to have healthy relationships and extend things like forgiveness. We have all the resources we need inside each one of us to reach this emotional maturity. When we look externally for love, validation, and acceptance, we get into tricky situations like addictions or reckless behavior. If we go outside of ourselves and our primary relationships for attention or reward, then we will be driven by a feeling of lack.

It's best to turn inward and figure out why we feel depleted and then do the work to cultivate what we need. When we take the time to become aware of our needs in this way, we allow ourselves to feel at peace, grounded, strong and connected. It is important to take time each day to focus on these feelings. It is also helpful to note our own negative emotions when we are suffering—anger, sadness, fear, hurt, guilt, rage, shame or grief. It is important to take time each day to understand when we are experiencing these feelings and seek to release them.

Within the Coaching modalities, there are trained professionals who specialize in mental and emotional release work. Being able to release negative emotions and the limiting beliefs that govern our decisions can be incredibly liberating and can bring enormous relief to those of us who have been repeating the same patterns over and over.

If you're ready to let go and finally be the fearless powerhouse you were meant to be, then see the Resource Center at the end of the book to get some coaching to help you move forward in new and profound ways. The quick and impactful sets of techniques featured in the Resource Center are the most effective I've seen.

In my personal experience, I came out of my coaching session a bolder, more fearless and resourceful person, ready to conquer the world. Whatever change you wish to bring about in your life, coaching will skyrocket you closer to it than ever before. You will understand why you keep repeating the same behaviors, why things have offended and hurt you so much and understand your fear strategies so you'll be able to release all the suffering you're holding on to. You'll also have an understanding of and the ability to move past the things that have been holding you back in life. Once you get beyond all your old patterns, you will have much more control over how things affect you in the future. When you begin to respond to situations differently you will finally have the power to *choose how you want to feel* and *how you want to respond* in any given situation.

Conscious Mind Vs. Subconscious Mind

All learning, behavior and change happen at the subconscious level. If you want to create a different outcome, you have to change your behaviors. To change your behaviors you have to change the way you think—consciously and subconsciously. The prime directive of the Subconscious Mind is to keep you safe, alive and is survival-based.

The gap between where you are now and where you want to be in all areas of your life causes you to chart some pretty unfamiliar territory. This is why we are in conflict between feelings of joy and abundance and the fear that can stop us when we go for our goals.

But the good news is the brain continually reorganizes itself by forming new neural connections throughout our lives. Everything we think, feel, do and experience gets encoded in our brains. Over time, the same set of thoughts, feelings, actions and experiences get hard-wired into patterns or states of being. That's why it's so important to become aware of what we are doing, thinking and feeling. It is possible to REWIRE a new state of being—one where we are truly thriving and able to accomplish anything, where we attract whatever we need.

TOOL # 1: Review Your Budget

Energy In must equal Energy Out in a given week to keep us feeling good, to feel like we are moving through life with ease. Think of it like a bank account for energy. You only have a finite amount to spend each week before you're tapped out. Your sense of willpower can give you an indication of how you're doing and make sure you don't make too many withdrawals.

You must find ways of restoring your energy in a given week by making deposits into your energy account before you start spending energy the next week or you'll be running on empty.

We all know what this feels like, don't we? You wake up Monday morning, exhausted, thinking about the week ahead and wondering how you're going to find the time or the capacity to do it all. Then you remember how many people need to be looked after or how many events and meetings you need to get to outside of your normal work-related activities. If we don't replenish, then we feel exhausted and run on empty, so we actually have less to give to the events and people in our life that matter. That includes not having enough energy to properly look after ourselves. Men and women both are socialized in different ways to believe this is not ok, but it is a very necessary part of wellbeing to learn how to do this.

Sarah, a CEO client of mine, had a beautiful life. A business she could run almost entirely virtual, lots of travel to beautiful destinations, a loving partner and a full social life when she wanted it or the ability to retreat and take some downtime when she needed. Her life was so well balanced, that she actually hadn't taken a vacation in two years. Her life felt so enjoyable and her work so fulfilling that even when she worked, she woke up feeling blessed and still had enough time to get to everything.

Until one day, we had a coaching call and she said she had been doing nothing differently, but some activities were leaving her more depleted than ever and she didn't have as much control over her diet and nutrition as before. She stated that when she went out to see friends, had dinner with some wine, it would sometimes take two days of recovery—eating a lot and sleeping a lot—for her to recharge.

We took a deeper look at the projects and the social events requiring her time and realized this latest branding project felt more taxing than her normal work. The rebranding of her whole company happened at a time when she was in a whole new city, so socializing wasn't just about seeing old friends and having a laugh. Socializing was now cultivating a new social group and vetting who she wanted in her life, versus just dinner. Both these elements in her life were requiring *more energy* and after a conversation about self-regulation, ego depletion and willpower, I suggested she dial back social activities just a bit until the project was complete.

While she didn't like the idea of stepping back from her social routine, her energy level stabilized and she was able to complete her work and feel less stressed. Her diet was also easier to manage and she had enough time to rest. A small, short-term change brought about so much more control and she flowed through life with ease and still had her needs met.

Success!

In the workbook, there's an exercise for you to review your energy budget in greater detail. For now, just notice the energy going out and energy coming back in. Notice the activities, the people, the events, the emotions that take energy and those that recharge you.

TOOL #2: Eliminate The Noise in Your Life

Once you assess your energy account you will notice if there are extraneous activities draining you of resources. It's time to stop engaging in activities and spending time with people that don't bring value to your life and drain you of your energy.

This is another tool for developing self-awareness. Start by being conscious of how you're feeling in each moment—Where are you? What are you doing? Who are you with? Then begin asking the following questions:

Do I feel at peace, happy, calm?

Does each person here make me feel at ease or is it challenging to be around them?

Am I truly enjoying what I'm doing with my time?

What is right about this situation?

What is wrong about this situation?

What about this situation does not resonate for me or make me feel like I'm living my best life?

Like I said before, my two favorite words are happy and easy. They are the gauges I use to measure whether people fit into my social circle and into my life. You might want to try the same metric for weeding people and situations out of your life that are depleting your energy bank account.

"Just as someone's bad mood can rub off on you, positivity, too, may spread," says Nicholas Christakis, professor of medical sociology, who has researched the concept of "emotional contagion" within the larger context of social networks. His findings have shown that happiness may be a collective phenomenon—having a happy friend who lives within a mile of you, for example, appears to increase the probability that you will be happy as well. In collaboration with James Fowler at the University of California at San Diego, Christakis found similar effects for the spread of happiness between next door neighbors, siblings that live nearby, and spouses—so that good feelings continue to move from person to person, even when there's no longer a direct connection to the original Pollyanna."[38]

If you're taking the time to find your way to happiness, then *you have a right to choose* what and with whom you choose to spend your time. Many people feel obligated to family members or old friends that require a lot of us. If there's an activity, social scene or a person that makes you feel drained, just notice it for now. Understand you get to choose how much time and energy you give away. Just don't engage. In the workbook, you'll get to do this work in more detail. For now, just start paying attention to the things that require your energy in a given week.

Just like when you make time to do a spring cleaning of your house or closet, it's time to really examine your life and ask yourself what brings you joy and what is just taking up space? Draw healthy boundaries so you have enough time to look after yourself and those that matter most.

Know that you absolutely have the right to choose the people and activities in your life. Choosing to spend time in situations that leave you feeling uplifted will strengthen your ability to stay in a state of calm and will give you greater energy.

TOOL #3:
Balance Your Budget, Balance Your Life

Just like doing a spring cleaning of your house or closet, it's time to really examine your life and ask yourself what brings you joy and what's just taking up space. Ask yourself some of these questions:

How can you revise your schedule so you aren't at zero in your energy account at the end of the week?

What small changes can you make so you aren't running on empty?

What changes can you make so that you are depositing energy back into your balance each week?

What are some of the activities that restore and deplete your energy?

Common sources are:

- Getting enough sleep (6-8 hours minimum)
- A balanced diet
- Regular exercise
- Support from family and friends
- Spending time alone - with no demands for your time and energy

As you learn to do this assessment, put it into practice more regularly. When you gain this awareness you will find you're naturally calmer, less stressed and able to experience more joy in each day because you are better able to be truly present.

In the world of science, we like empirical evidence. Empirical evidence is defined as the information received by means of the senses, particularly by observation and documentation of patterns and behavior, usually through experimentation.

In the world of coaching, we like to ask "How will you know when you have it?" In other words, what is your evidence procedure? In the workbook, you'll get to go through a detailed exercise of energy inputs and outputs and you will have an opportunity to balance your energy budget.

For now, here are some indications that you are in balance mentally, emotionally and physically.

- You wake up feeling more rested
- You have more even energy throughout the day
- You are more in control of your emotional state
- Your stress level seems manageable
- Your sleep quality is improving
- You have better willpower as needed

Week 3:

W = WHAT DO YOU NEED?

"Your job is to fill your own cup, so it overflows.
Then, you can serve others joyfully from your saucer."

—**Lisa Nichols,** motivational speaker,
founder of Motivating the Masses

This week we will examine your needs in *a whole new way* and redefine your life so you can have those needs met and really feel as though you are *thriving*! As we do this, you will also notice you are shifting your mindset so you can create more of what you want in your life.

Most of us go through life without anyone ever asking us what makes us happy. A parent may have asked when we were deeply upset about what we needed in that moment, but very few of us grew up with anyone really asking:

What do you need?

What do you need to feel your best?

What do you need to feel good about yourself and your life?

What do you need so that you feel loved and cherished?

What do you need so that you feel like you are important, that your needs matter, that YOU matter?

What do you need to have a life filled with peace or laughter or excitement?

What makes you feel the most alive and engaged in your life?

As a result, most of us just wander through life as though it's happening to us and we're just doing our best to navigate our way through it. We may have had some guidance when we were too little to fend for ourselves, but ever since we established our independence, we just meandered through life—first through school and childhood, then adolescence, maybe when choosing a major for college or university. Then we just swam through all that too as well as the life events that happened during those years. After we started a job or career, we figured out how to manage our time between work and non-work-related activities.

But how many of us really stopped and asked—*Am I happy?* Let alone—*What do I need to be happy?*

Most of us, if not all of us, go through life just trying to do our best and go along with what's expected of us—be a good friend, daughter or son, mother or father, co-worker, boss. About 25 years ago, when I started down the path of self-development and the study of success, a man asked me a simple question—What makes you happy?

Tongue-tied, I searched for words to describe my answer. I found the experience of answering his question shocking. I hadn't, before that moment, considered myself to be UN-happy, yet I couldn't say definitively what made me happy.

What Is Happiness?

There is no simple answer. Happiness can't be found in any one place, although many of us try. It can't be found exclusively in any one of our four bodies—the spiritual, mental, emotional, or the physical.

- If happiness could only be found in the spiritual realm, then a daily routine of meditation should serve all our needs and make us happy.

- If happiness could only be found in the mind or mental body, then learning how to master our thoughts alone would work.
- If happiness could be achieved in the emotional body alone, then learning Emotional Intelligence and self-regulation would be all that was needed.
- If happiness could only be found in our physical body—then a simple diet and exercise program would suffice. We could therefore ensure that we are doing all the right things to produce the right neurochemicals.

We all know people who drive hard in one of these areas. People who work out 24/7 trying to control their physique or people who study so much that they accumulate many doctorate degrees and professional success. While they are noble endeavors, many of these paths don't lead to happiness. All four bodies need to be aligned in order to achieve happiness—the Spiritual, Mental, Emotional and Physical.

Over the last few years, working as a Happiness and Success Coach, I would ask the same question to my clients—What makes you happy? I found some people could answer it easily in some areas of their lives, but not in others. It occurred to me that most of us don't really take the time to know what makes us happy, and when we do, we don't know how to find it. To help my clients meet this challenge, I created a Needs Analysis to help them define their needs easily. It's impossible to design a life you love, then put some goals around that, if you don't even know if that life will bring you closer to happiness. So let's start with your needs.

Needs Analysis—Center, Ground and Recharge

Don't worry about the details for now, as we will get into a detailed exercise in the workbook. This week, I'd like to start the NEEDS ANALYSIS by asking you to ponder this question—

What do you NEED in order to be happy?

In other words, if being happy meant you were your most vibrant self, living a meaningful life, what do you need in your life every day or every week? Each of us has different needs that must be fulfilled in order for us to feel like we are happy and thriving. It's similar to having a car with a full tank of gas and a fresh tune-up. When your car is looked after, it runs well and it performs more efficiently. So do we.

When we don't take the time to meet our needs, we feel depleted, and this can cause us to feel overwhelmed. If we let this go for too long, we start to feel exhausted, stressed, dissatisfied and generally unhappy, always living in dis-EASE, a state of dissatisfaction can then permeate every area of our lives, from school to work to our home lives, social lives, relationships, sleep quality and even our health.

This is particularly true for busy parents who are usually so focused on juggling time and energy for everyone in the family that they forget their own needs. After some time, *they begin to believe that their needs are not important* and then they begin to believe their happiness is not important. When we get used to not having our needs met it causes us to fall into and get used to a dangerous place called the comfort zone.

Comfort Zone

This is where most people spend their lives. We actually get to a point where we stop *allowing* ourselves to want the things that make us happy because we've not had them for so long. We may not even have an awareness of the things that make us happy or how we deny ourselves from having them. Instead, we stop negotiating for what feels good and relax into what we have, even if we are not fulfilled.

It becomes exhausting to lose ourselves and bury our needs. When you are finally ready to make a change, the results of this behavior can show up in many ways:

- You're tired of being tired
- You're feeling like you're not as healthy as you'd like to be
- You feel like you want deeper connections with the people in your life
- You think you could make more money, have more financial freedom
- You want more time for yourself and more energy to do what you enjoy
- You think your life could be more satisfying, more exciting, *more something*
- You feel like your life lacks excitement and passion but you don't know why

Whenever you become aware that you need more from life and are interested in seeking it out, you have been living in the comfort zone. Real and meaningful change will only occur once you start to examine your needs in a whole new way and then make changes in your life to have those needs met. This may require small changes for some needs and bigger changes for others. To get out of the comfort zone, get your needs met, and bring about powerful and positive change in your life, you need to *get comfortable being uncomfortable.* Even making one small change will help you feel excited again and will help make it easier to get the rest of your needs met.

Ready for Change

Let's take a moment to celebrate the fact that you're here! It's no accident that you've picked up this book and are reading this passage. If it resonates with you in any way, then you will have seen, heard or felt some shift. You may have just let out a big exhale because this sounds like the change you've been seeking without realizing it. You may have seen areas of your life that could be far more exhilarating! Or you may have just felt some relief to know that you can finally figure out what's been missing AND learn how to have the life you've always wanted!

YOU ARE READY FOR CHANGE. You are now ready to step into a happier, more powerful version of you. As a coach and someone who devotes her life to helping others live to their fullest potential, I am thrilled for you and honored to be part of your journey.

One Size Doesn't Fit All

The first thing we need to do is figure out what your NEEDS are. It's different for each of us and what we need each day can change. For example, some days we need to be energized, other days we need to be focused, and some days we need to do only the necessary and take time to be still and recharge. Much like our diets, what we need is fairly consistent, but what we feel like each day may differ from moment to moment. And you are the only one who can know your particular needs.

Isn't it irritating when you speak to someone about what's lacking or what you think you need in your life and they go off on some longwinded lecture about what you should do because it worked for them?

Over many years of asking my clients what works for them and hearing people share their newfound wisdom about their needs anecdotally, I learned that what works for one does NOT work for everyone. What my friends or family members need is not the same as what works for me. Each of us must explore the unique formula that really makes us feel fulfilled. We are all so very different. There is no one-size-fits-all when it comes to finding our joy.

A Steady Diet

We are each unique in our set of needs and while, overall, the needs we each have are consistent, the list can change from day to day. For example, if you feel wonderful after having a night to yourself or a great workout or a day fully engaged with your kids or a wonderful dinner with your partner, then that is a consistent need that needs to be fulfilled. However, one day I may feel the need to be social and another day I know I need to relax and unwind and have some quiet time to recharge. It's important that you start thinking about what you need on a daily and weekly basis. If you don't fully know, just start paying attention to what feels good and pretty soon, your list will take shape. Ask yourself, what do I need this week, this day, this hour?

Your Needs Are Non-Negotiable

In my studies in Neuroscience and NLP, Neurolinguistic Programming, essentially the study of successful people, I learned that not only are your needs important to identify but they are also *non-negotiable.* If you decide to negotiate around them, the cost is huge. When you don't have your needs met over time, you will start to feel tired, uncomfortable, irritable, impatient, dissatisfied and unhappy.

Most of us are unaware of how to define our needs because our needs get lost in the shuffle of our busy lives and our connection to them can even disappear. Most of the time, instead of acknowledging our needs and setting up boundaries around them, we overextend ourselves. This leaves us feeling stretched all the time, to the point we don't feel there is enough time to do everything that is important in our life. To make matters worse, we don't want to impose ourselves on others, so we become afraid to push our healthy boundaries.

So how can we possibly ensure our needs are met with our families, partners, spouses, colleagues, friends and ourselves?

Many of us even feel like it's selfish to take the time to ask for what we need. But self-care is never selfish. Meeting your needs is the best way to feel like your most vibrant self. By feeling your best, you honor those around you by being able to respond to them attentively. By letting others know where your boundaries are, you are more in control of your emotional state and actually more available to others in the long run.

Why not learn how to communicate your needs to others and then teach this to your partner, your kids, families and your team at work and make sure everyone is happy and thriving? Can you imagine how the world would change if we took care of ourselves before taking care of others? If you are feeling your best and those around you are feeling their best, we would be more joyful, more at peace, more connected, more content and in a better state of health. So how do we get there?

Breaking Down Your Needs

Once you take some time to review your needs and notice what's been missing, then we will define a plan to have it all. Because you can have it all! Maybe not all on one day or maybe you won't be able to have everything you need in a week, because life happens and it will sometimes interrupt our flow. But the key to happiness is defining what makes you happy so you can experience more of those moments.

In order to help you define your needs, I'd like you to break them down into the following categories and measure those categories in hours or events per week—Physical, Social, Mental & Intellectual, Emotional, Financial, Soulful & Spiritual.

Let's consider each category and get to the heart of what you need—

Physical

How much food, water, exercise, sleep and fresh air do you need to really feel great? Fresh air seems so simple. Yet, when I lived in Canada, February was the coldest month and you were lucky if you were able to be outside comfortably for any length of time. So it is something to consider. How do you need your home and your work environment to look so you can feel peaceful, calm and at ease? Do you need things to be tidy and well organized so that you also have clarity of mind? Do you like it filled with memories and warmth, because that's what feels nurturing for you? Do you get enough physical space or time alone?

If I drink 2-3 liters of water a day I feel like I have boundless energy. If I sleep 7-8 hours, I feel wonderful. Others may need 10 hours of sleep. I also need to walk along the ocean to feel my best. Start to pay attention to what FEELS GOOD in your life. This is your list, so think about what activities and experiences make you feel the most energized, vibrant, and alive. Write a few of them down.

Social

Do you feel great when you are able to see friends, family, and engage with your community? Do you need to be social one night a week or do you need to socialize more often? Do you prefer being social on your own, or do you prefer socializing with your partner and kids? Do you need more or fewer people in your life? What's the perfect combination of social activities for you so you can have your needs met?

What feels GOOD to YOU? Are you someone who feels comfortable to go out alone and explore the world? Or do you need a wingman with you at all times? Once you become aware of how much social activity you need and what kind you enjoy, you can begin to negotiate how to support your social needs with the people in your life so you can all get what you need.

Mental & Intellectual

What sort of mental, intellectual, and creative stimulation do you need in order to feel excited and inspired? This may come from books, podcasts, documentaries, films, galleries, exhibits, engaging in stimulating conversation or it may come in another form. Take time to note when you feel you're most engaged, interested or inspired.

I have one client that gets lost watching YouTube videos. They're all instructional videos, so it speaks to his love of learning and he can do this when he doesn't feel like reading a book. That's not for everyone. I have another client who is constantly learning. He's always engaged in learning a new language or mastering a new skill and it makes him feel alive to have something that's just his to focus on—away from work, away from family. Take time to note when you feel most engaged, interested or inspired. Take note also of how often you need to be stimulated in this way. Is it every day? Is it one evening or a few hours per week? Also, begin asking yourself, how will I know when I am having this need met? How will I feel when it's not met and I'm craving some mental stimulation?

We talked about neuroplasticity earlier—it's the brain's ability to form new neural connections and create lasting change. Well, here's a great way to prevent cognitive decline as you get older. *Learning IS neuroplasticity.* By constantly learning, we're constantly allowing our brain to generate new neurons—a sort of workout for the brain.

Aside from the benefit of neuroplasticity, there are many other benefits of learning something new. The sheer mastery of a new skill lights up the brain's reward centers and makes us feel more confident, rewrites our history of success, and increases our sense of capability. More on this in the workbook.

"If Plan A fails, remember there are 25 more letters."

—Chris Guillebeau, author of *The Happiness of Pursuit*

We are a work in progress—learning about ourselves and the world around us can be incredibly stimulating. I need to always be learning something. In the last few years, I've been building a business so there was much to learn about creating a mobile app, branding, marketing, social media and the world of mind/body connection, personal transformation, and success coaching.

New information and learning new skills stimulated my mind and made me happy. At a prior point in my life, when I worked a 9-to-5 job, I was happiest when learning something creative, so I took painting, dance, and language classes. My happiness comes from finding something to master or something that feels therapeutic and disconnects me from everyday activities, allowing me to discover something new and inspiring. This could be anything from learning to cook a new and spectacular meal or reading a book on a subject that interests me. Whatever interests you, take note of what you need to stimulate and challenge you intellectually and educationally.

Emotional (Affection, Love, Sex)

What type of support do you need? Do you need time with friends? Better communication with your loved ones? How much sexual activity do you like and how do you like it? Do you need a little affection or a lot? What is your love language?

Gary Chapman, in his book *The 5 Love Languages,* spells out five unique ways we speak our love and need it returned to us—words of affirmation, quality time, receiving gifts, acts of service, and physical touch. Do you know what love language you speak? Are you expressing love and receiving love in an optimal way for you? Do you know the love language of your partner? Do you feel seen, heard and valued in your relationships? Start to become aware of what FEELS GOOD in your relationships.

Here are the 5 Love Languages, how to communicate them and what actions to take:[39]

- Words of Affirmation
  - Encourage, affirm, appreciate, empathize.
  - Listen actively.
  - Send an unexpected note, text, or card.
  - Genuinely encourage, and often.
- Physical Touch
  - Non-verbal—use body language and touch to express love hug, kiss, hold hands, show physical affection often.
  - Make intimacy a thoughtful priority.
- Receiving Gifts
  - Thoughtfulness, make your spouse a priority, speak purposefully.
  - Give thoughtful gifts and gestures. Small things matter in a big way.
  - Express gratitude when receiving a gift.
- Quality Time
  - Uninterrupted and focused conversations. One-on-one time is critical.
  - Create special moments together, take walks and do small things with your partner. Weekend getaways are huge.
- Acts of Service
  - Use action phrases like "I'll help..." They want to know you're with them, partnered with them.
  - Do chores together or make them breakfast in bed. Go out of your way to help alleviate their daily workload.

After you know how you need to be loved and how to love your partner in return, get really specific on what excites you the most. One of my coaches called this the "What Rocks You list" and I love that! What do you need in your relationship that would rock your world? And yes, YOU DO NEED IT, so PUT IT ON THE LIST. If we are here, taking the time to create a life we can be excited about, then stop playing small or feeling like we don't deserve it.

YOU CAN HAVE EVERYTHING YOUR HEART DESIRES! If you need time to go big, then for now, just pretend and think about what sets your heart on fire and lights you up! Write. It. Down. Every little thing that makes you feel safe, protected, valued, looked after, loved, supported, gorgeous, desired, cherished and adored needs to be on your list!

By the way, once you can define what you'd like to show up in your life, it starts showing up! So get ready. If you take the time to articulate it to the universe, it might just show up! Whether you are in a relationship or not, start to be really specific and communicate your needs. When you do, amazing things start to happen.

Financial

In order to feel like you have no worries, get really specific about what you need to have financially to feel secure.

How much money do you need to live on each month?
How much do you want to play with for entertainment each month?
What is your necessary budget?
What is your fantasy budget?

If you have a differential between your necessary and fantasy budget, you can draw up a plan to work toward and achieve the ultimate lifestyle that is *balanced and playful.* If you don't clearly define what you need, it will be difficult to achieve because you'll always be left wanting more. Knowing how much you need and want each month can help you see whether where you are is very fortunate, or it can help define your goals.

When you achieve them, you'll be able to take a breath and be happy about your accomplishment because you have what you need. So you will break the cycle of negative thought that leaves you always needing or wanting more. If you can define how much you need so that you have your bills covered, your playtime covered, your family and your future covered, then the rest is all gravy. So take some time to work out what this is for you and run the numbers. Once you have a clear view of these amounts, you can take a breath and feel at ease that you either have it or have a plan to work toward achieving it.

In the workbook in the next section, you'll get to imagine your dream life, but for now, begin to think about what you need to get into place to meet your financial goals. It's more about knowing what amount of money will reduce your stress and give you the ability to live a decent quality of life. It all depends on what makes you happy. If you prefer a simple lifestyle, plan for that. If you want luxury, then begin to imagine what you might need. Draw up a plan to work toward and achieve the ultimate lifestyle that is balanced and playful. If you don't clearly define what you need, it will be difficult to achieve because you'll always be wanting more.

Once you have a clear view of the lifestyle you imagine, you can take a breath and feel at ease because you will either have achieved that lifestyle or you will have a plan to work toward achieving it.

Soulful & Spiritual

What makes you feel calm, serene, at peace, and grounded? This doesn't only come from prayer or the practice of your faith. What adds meaning to your life? What are the things you need to feed your soul? For me, being by the water calms me. I look out on the ocean each morning from my living room, and the energy of the sea fills me with a sense of calm—a spiritual moment. It grounds me, and helps me feel at peace. I also need to meditate each morning to quiet my mind. It gives me clarity, focus, energy, and helps me accomplish amazing things in my day and in my life. If I miss it for a day, I can feel it. If I do it later in the day, it's not as enjoyable and it's not as easy to find that stillness that is so vital to begin my day with ease.

Although meditation and I had a bumpy ride earlier on, it has now become my favorite part of the day. Now I wake up, shower, brew some coffee and sit for twenty minutes or more. I start by thinking *how I want to feel—peaceful, calm, happy.* A smile actually forms on my lips as I begin. Almost immediately the tension from my neck and shoulders release. Then I focus on my day. What do I need to accomplish today? I imagine everything coming together easily. Then I focus on the other areas of my life: love, relationships, friendships, career, health and anything that comes to mind. Some people meditate like me by just sitting quietly. Maybe for you, meditation could be taking a yoga class or engaging in some form of exercise that connects your mind and body and has you focus on your breath.

Also doing philanthropic work and engaging in activities to help others makes me feel like I'm fulfilling my purpose here and makes me feel content as well. If you already know your WHY, and you have a life of meaning and purpose, then keep doing what you're doing. If you don't, then just begin to think about what would make your life meaningful. We get more into this later in the book. As you can see I satisfy my spiritual side with a combination of things that soothe and feed my spirit. Start to think about what you need to feel fulfilled, to feel like you have purpose, to quiet your mind, and help you to feel calm, happy, grounded.

A Note About Health

Your body has supported you well (hopefully) for all these years. It's important to look after it so it can continue to offer that support. We've all had days or years when we didn't eat well, didn't hydrate adequately or sleep enough, and even worse, downright polluted our bodies—and still they continued to look after us. Be mindful that your body has served you well, even when you haven't taken the best care of it, and start to look after it now.

It's not about having the perfect body—it's about being happy, healthy and strong so your body can sustain you for the coming years. We put premium fuel in our cars and get regular oil changes so they operate well. Why don't we look after our bodies in the same way? We need optimal fuel to have optimal energy.

Here's how you can tell that you're running on empty:

- you wake up exhausted
- you can't control the amount of food you eat
- you crave sweets more often than you'd like
- you have frequent indigestion, stomach aches or headaches
- your breathing may be tight from time to time, or regularly
- you don't have consistent energy throughout the day. Your energy level peaks and drops, so you reach for caffeine or sugar or feel like taking a nap.

If you have any or all of the symptoms above, then you probably need to look at your nutrition, activity level and sleep habits. Diets don't work over the long haul, but making small changes to optimize your energy, strength and stamina will work over time to bring about the change you need.

Making Time

Take an inventory of how you spend your time, who you spend it with, who supports what you need, and check in to assess whether you communicate your needs to those around you. Start having conversations about needs with the people in your life so you all understand each other's needs and can support each other in meeting them. Once you have that, then you can plan your days, weeks, and months around everyone's needs.

For example, if you're in a relationship and you're social and your partner is less so, find a way to negotiate how you spend your time so that each of your needs are met. If you have children and need some time to yourself, create a way with your spouse, partner or friends so you have some alone time when needed.

After this week, you'll feel a powerful change in your life when you recognize your needs and have begun to create space in your life to accommodate them. I know you're ready to start living life more successfully. You're ready to feel more at peace, focused, and joyful. The more you honor your needs, you retrain your brain to stay in the positive emotional states of calm, peace, and happiness, where you can feel proud of yourself. The more time you spend in these positive states—feeling like you are truly thriving—the less stress, exhaustion and dissatisfaction will have a hold on you. Every time you honor your need, you rewire your brain for greater happiness.

Creating a NEW Neurology

We need to create a NEW neurology to get to the next level of happiness in our lives. As we have seen this week, we need to align the Spiritual, Mental, Emotional and Physical Bodies and keep our awareness of all four of them to bring us true happiness. When we do, we create a space for happiness and abundance to flow into our life because we have weakened our old programming that is based on fear and survival. Awareness and balance chart our course for a new way of living.

When we acknowledge this new way of living—where we feel comfortable owning, communicating and receiving our needs—we raise our vibration to one of love and abundance. The rubber meets the road with our needs this week when we hone our ability to acknowledge our needs as non-negotiable.

This cycle of creating a new neurology aligns the Spiritual, Mental, Emotional & Physical bodies by creating a space for happiness and abundance while weakening our old programming. The following tools will help you to make this a reality.

TOOL #1:
Pay Attention To What Makes You Feel Most Alive

Think of the moments in life when you felt the most excited, energized and alive. Those were moments during or immediately after you had your needs met! It could have happened during a great workout, or strolling outdoors as you breathed in the fresh air and took in the sights and sounds of nature. It could've been during a beautiful quiet night to yourself or when you went out with friends. Take a minute now to think of a few of these moments in your life.

For example, after a great workout, I feel completely energized—strong, capable, like I can achieve anything! My cheeks are flushed and fresh oxygen pumps through me. My posture seems better and I notice the feeling of more confidence as I walk. Happy little endorphins dance inside my body. I feel totally happy and alive, calm and relaxed—really feeling *good*. Sometimes I'll get home after a great night out with friends and just feel exhilarated. Other times, I'll attend an event or a social dinner and come home exhausted, and maybe the following week the same events will energize me.

Occasionally, I'll take a night to myself when I turn my phone off and do whatever feels good at that moment—make a nice dinner, put on my favorite music, maybe take a bath, read a book, or watch a movie, allowing my body to rest. Afterward, I feel totally relaxed as I climb into bed and realize the wonderful feeling of taking the time for solitude. When I'm quiet and allow myself to be still, I'm aware of how I interact with the world. Stillness gives me a solid place to notice what works and what doesn't in my life.

Take time to be still. Get in tune with how you interact with the world in this space.

When your needs are fulfilled—it feels right. It feels *good*. It centers, grounds, recharges and calms you. It is so very necessary that we find the time to have our needs met to flourish in life and feel a deeper sense of satisfaction.

You need to get comfortable being uncomfortable to really bring about powerful and positive change in your life. Isn't it a relief to know that you aren't alone when you feel unfulfilled? Probably everyone feels this way at some point. It's just that when we don't know how or aren't able to take the time to really examine the heart of the problem—getting our needs met—we all default to acting like we've got everything figured out.

When we don't prioritize our needs and take this important time for solitude, we use up all our energy in activity without refilling our reserves. Remember, energy is like a cache or a bank account—energy in must equal energy out. If we don't replenish, it's like running on an empty tank. We feel tired, depleted and unable to cope with everything we need to attend to. If we let this go for too long, we start to feel exhausted, stressed.

With this guide to deconstructing and examining your life, you have the information you need to make small changes that will help you really feel excited again. When you begin to seek this new life where your needs are front and center, you will uncover areas of your life that can be far more exhilarating! The workbook has exercises for you to discover ways to easily figure out what's been missing AND learn how to have the life you've always wanted! Let's begin by becoming aware of your unique needs.

TOOL #2:
Define Your Core Needs

I can imagine you might be saying—*Sure, of course, thanks for the sage advice, I need more sleep. How do I do that when my life is so busy?*

Well, you may not have all your needs met all of the time, because life is sometimes busy and sometimes messy. What you can do is *start by understanding what your needs are*. From there, you can start to reorganize your life to have more of what you need. In order to help you define your needs, you also must quantify *how much* you need. In the workbook, you'll get a chance to work more on becoming aware of your needs.

For now, just take a look at your notes from the Need Analysis earlier in the chapter and compile them into one list so you can see your needs clearly in the following categories—

Physical—How much food, water, exercise, sleep, fresh air, do you need to feel great?

Social—Are you a social butterfly? How often do you like to see friends and family? Are you comfortable socializing alone or with a partner or friend?

Mental & Intellectual—What sort of mental, intellectual and creative stimulation do you need in order to feel excited and inspired—books, podcasts, documentaries, films, galleries or exhibits, engaging in stimulating conversation?

New information and learning new skills stimulates the mind. What might satisfy your passions? Painting, dance and language classes? History classes or acquiring a new skill?

Emotional (Affection, Love, Sex)—Are you having your needs met in your primary relationship with yourself? In your secondary relationship with your partner? Are you getting the support and type of support that you need?

Financial—In order to feel like you have no worries and anxiety about the future, get really specific on what you need to have financial security.

Soulful & Spiritual—What are your spiritual needs? What makes you feel calm, serene, at peace, grounded?

TOOL #3: How Can You Have More Of Your Needs Met More Often?

Once you have a clear picture of what your needs are, *put them on your calendar.* When you make a few simple changes (yes, it's as simple as that), like committing to spending time on your needs, then you can live life with ease. You will hear yourself exhale and feel more relaxed. Almost immediately, you will experience instant relief knowing that you've decided to get off the hamster wheel of everyone else's expectations for your life and instead live the life that makes you happier. Once you've identified your needs and scheduled them, life becomes immensely more satisfying and can be lived with greater ease.

Week 4:

I = IMAGINE & VISUALIZE A NEW FUTURE

So far, we've learned the importance of tending to each of the four bodies—Spiritual, Mental, Emotional and Physical—and a bit about how they're interconnected. Then we learned how to quiet the mind in order to reduce stress and retrain the brain and body back to calm. Next, we learned about self-regulation and why it's necessary to conserve our energy from week to week. After that, we also went through some tools to help you be in better control of your environment so you can create a space for more peace and balance to show up in your life. In the last section, we did a deep dive into what really makes you feel most alive, so you're truly enjoying a life that is meaningful and exciting.

This week, we'll go a bit deeper into what's important to you so that you can include more of your core values into the new life you will get to construct. Why does this matter? If you think of your needs as all of the elements that go into building your dream home (for example, the natural light you want, whether it overlooks the water or is surrounded by trees—the things that make you feel good), then your core values are the foundation of this new home. And you get to be the architect.

What are your core values? Once we have a clearer sense of them, we'll have enough material to start creating a new vision and a new life that truly moves you! When we've done the work to erase old patterns, find our peace, regulate our emotions and reduce the noise we'll have arrived at a place where we can design something new. This is where you get to be the architect of your new life.

Are you ready to begin? Let's do it!

This week begins with cultivating a deeper sense of self-awareness so you have more clarity about what's working well in your life and getting rid of what is no longer in line with your values. Once you start to develop a clearer image of what you want to create in your life and how you want to feel, then you can begin taking action by imagining a new future. As you do this, you begin to *rewire the brain toward your new life* and hardwire a new mindset so that your reality aligns too.

Remember, many of us have spent so much time focusing on what's missing, that we've created a normal pattern of concentrating on what's lacking. To counterbalance this old pattern, we need to install a new pattern where our thoughts, feelings and behaviors link together to create a new outcome, a new pattern. We've spent so much time training ourselves in the old way of being. Now, we get to choose a new way of being that's more aligned with what's important to us. Again, one size does not fit all. You might need adventure while your partner craves routine, so it's necessary to understand each of your core values.

What Are Your Values?

Let's take a deeper look at the things that matter to you most. What are the overlying themes in your life now and what would you like more of? Your **values** are what's important to you. Like air, you can't live without them. If you can determine your values, then you can shift your priorities. Whether you are true to your values can be a good gauge for how you feel you are doing in life.

Just like the section on needs, we are not usually asked, *What's important to you?* So, if we are not clear on what's important to us and our values it's likely we're not ensuring that these themes permeate the important areas of our life.

But, what is a personal value? Values can be hard to discern when we aren't used to sorting them out. Our values guide and motivate us. For example, you may value honesty and need to speak your mind to feel fulfilled. When you don't speak up about your truth, you feel disappointed in yourself. Or maybe you value kindness and help others and generously give of your time to help those in need. Adventurers value intrepid experiences over safe or conventional choices. People who love security would make different choices. These are just a few examples.

Everyone is different. What makes you happy may be different from what makes your brothers, sisters, friends and coworkers happy. This week it's time to use the skills you developed in the first three weeks to get quiet and listen in to your own mind.

Take some time to think about your top values. Do you find ways to really incorporate them into your life?

Let's break it down

Use the list below to see if any of these personal values speak to you as themes or guiding principles that really light you up in your personal life. In this book, we are mainly interested in your personal experience so we will focus on those. You can also look at values that relate to your business, social, political or world views. For now, just see if any of these speak to you personally or if any have left you feeling conflicted if you didn't have them in your life.

Adventurer

For example, I had a client named Patricia, who was married to a wealthy man. Before marriage, Patrica was a successful journalist and entrepreneur and had a beautiful and adventurous life. Her mother taught her to always be self-sufficient, so she could always have the ability to look after herself and make choices in her life. And she did! A very full life, great circle of friends, lots of social activity and travel to interesting and exotic places.

She waited a long time to meet the right person before she got married. When she met Troy, she thought she'd found her counterpart—smart, savvy, fun, adventurous, social. They had a lot of love between them and enjoyed their time together. When it came time for them to enter into a commitment, the timing was such that Troy needed to travel cross country for his new role. In order to support the relationship, they discussed perhaps for a short while, she would dial back on her work and be more available for him and enjoy their life together.

Patricia didn't realize until later that when she made the choice to be supportive of her partner, she also gave up her autonomy. Autonomy, unbeknownst to her, was a driving force in her life and she drew strength from her ability to look after herself. When her life changed where someone else paid most of the bills, the balance of the relationship shifted.

It wasn't only financial. There were emotional expectations that shifted too. What's important here, was that she was unaware that she had just given her power away and even more unaware of how miserable it would make her. Over a period of time, she tried to convince herself to step into this new role, but ultimately it was uncomfortable for her and she lost a bit of what made her this gorgeous, bold, exciting woman to be around.

She slowly started to lose her shine and even slipped into a bit of depression. Had Patricia and her husband understood the financial arrangements and how they affected their values, they could easily have been renegotiated, and it's likely they could have made their marriage work. Instead, she vied for a bit of her independence back, and he was more comfortable in a codependent relationship. Only one possibility showed up for them—they were not meeting each other's needs and no longer able to make each other happy. They decided to end their marriage, even though there was still so much love between them.

Patricia realized a huge life lesson—to stay true to herself and never give up that autonomy again! As she moves forward in life, Patricia now understands the importance of having a true partnership—filled with mutual love, respect, admiration, and with someone strong enough to feel secure when she stands on her own and is her fierce self. Losing that relationship also taught her the importance of a deeper self-love and she is happier and more at peace now than ever before.

Wild child

I have another client, we'll call her Sonia, who was the most free-spirited creature I ever met. She made her own rules, lived by her own code and was a young woman in the prime of life. She chose careers that gave her flexibility and freedom, and would rather poke herself in the eye than take a 9-to-5 desk job which would keep her in one environment with the same group of people day in and day out. If you're cringing at the idea of someone like this, then you're likely on the other end of the spectrum and someone that loves stability, safety, routine. There's no right or wrong and no judgment in what values you have. They are a part of who you are and what makes you unique and special, so honor whatever shows up for you.

But, back to Sonia. She was an extreme extrovert and as highly social as you could imagine. She is the sort of person that can create warmth and connection everywhere she goes, and she does. People just adore her. One day, she learned she was pregnant. Now this wild child was with child and about to bring new life into the world. Processing her new reality, she went from single girl to being in a committed relationship and an expectant mom.

Okay, she thought, *I'm going to stay as calm and peaceful as I possibly can for the sake of this child and I know I will be all right.* While this was unplanned, her relationship gave her some comfort. It kept her in good shape until the beautiful baby arrived and even during the first three months while she navigated being a new mom. Then one day she arrived at my office, flustered and emotional.

She started to tell me how she didn't really have a moment to fully develop from a single girl in the dating world to a woman in a committed relationship, let alone process the fact that she was a new mother. She loved her new partner, adored her child and enjoyed being a mother. It wasn't as if she was pining for her old single-girl days. But if you recall, it was like someone flipped a switch and abandoned that wild child.

She felt frustrated and confused. After some digging, she began to realize, at her core, she values freedom and adventure so much, that it really defines her. But she didn't know how they would fit into her new reality. So we worked together to define new ways for her core values to exist in her new paradigm.

She didn't want to quit working altogether, as she still needs the mental stimulation and energy she draws from her work. She needed to have conversations with her partner about how they spend time together so that she can still include adventure and freedom in her new life. She found the perfect partner. He fully supported her needs and was very understanding. In fact, she was finding new ways of allowing her authentic self to exist, so she could feel her best for herself, her partner, and her child. Sonia is now happily finding and redefining her free, adventurous life as she goes, but feeling much happier and relieved that she didn't have to change who she was.

The importance of values

Another client craved and valued stability overall. Glen was an artist, dating a corporate executive named Beth. Beth was high energy, high performing, highly social but also enjoyed her solitude and quiet time, whether alone or with Glen. Early on in his life, Glen suffered some trauma when his father left at a young age, so he was not comfortable with change. He valued solitude and could take it or leave it if a social situation arose. He and Beth had a great connection, but Beth was definitely more spontaneous.

One spring Saturday, with no clear plans, they discussed how they'd like to spend the day. They decided on a long walk and then lunch. Just as they were leaving, Beth remembered she had something she needed to return at the mall and asked Glen if he minded a slight detour. So they got their long walk in, stopped to do a bit of shopping, at which point Glen's mood changed entirely and he sunk into a state for the rest of the day.

It took them days to figure out why such a small change in plans could have ruined an entire weekend, but I helped them realize *the simplicity of understanding the importance of values.* It came down to this—Glen, who values routine and stability, is far more comfortable if he knows what's going to happen in advance. When plans change, it triggers a feeling of not being in control, so he responds without realizing what's upsetting him. What he came to value was the stability of being in control of his life as much as possible.

Beth, who is one to go with the flow and loves the variety of spontaneity, changed plans on the fly, making him terribly uncomfortable. We figured out a way for them to have this discussion and resolve any future mishaps with ease. They are now living with a lot less tension in their relationship and happily keeping or changing plans as needed!

Have a look at the list below and just try each value on to see if it resonates for you. Ask yourself—*How important are each of these values to me? How would I feel if I didn't have this in my life?* As you go through the list, you'll start to discover areas of your personality that are more important than others and distinguish the values you cannot live without.

- [ ] Achievement
- [ ] Adventure
- [ ] Autonomy
- [ ] Compassion
- [ ] Courage
- [ ] Creativity
- [ ] Determination
- [ ] Excitement
- [ ] Friendship
- [ ] Freedom
- [ ] Health
- [ ] Honesty
- [ ] Independence
- [ ] Integrity
- [ ] Intelligence
- [ ] Justice
- [ ] Kindness
- [ ] Learning
- [ ] Love
- [ ] Peace
- [ ] Perfection
- [ ] Routine
- [ ] Security
- [ ] Simplicity
- [ ] Sincerity
- [ ] Spontaneity
- [ ] Success
- [ ] Understanding
- [ ] Wealth

Stop Focusing On Lack—Re-Focus On What You Have And The Future

Most of us spend a lot of time thinking about what we wish we had, what we'd like to have or what's missing in our lives in order for us to be happy. When we are focused on what is NOT in our lives, it can increase our drive and help us strive for a better life. But it also takes unnecessary energy as we ruminate on how we would like things to be different. Lack *keeps us in a place where something is more demanding of our time and energy than is necessary.*

Stress is how your body responds to any type of demand or threat. When you sense danger—whether it is real or imagined—the body's defenses kick into high gear in a rapid, automatic process known as the "fight-or-flight" reaction or "stress response." We should have the ability to return to our calmer rest-and-digest state quickly after a stressful event has occurred. But because life is so busy, we have strengthened our stress response and weakened our calmer state. We have even weakened our ability to return to calm quickly, if at all. When we are focused on what's missing, we are essentially keeping our bodies in a state of di-*stress.*

Instead, if you focus on *how much you already have*, on the blessings in your life, and the feelings associated with those, then you begin to allow your brain to enter its calmer state easily. For example, as you focus on how lucky you are to be alive, to have your health, your family, or the good things in your life, and really allow yourself to *feel* into those moments, you're embodying the very emotions that come with those thoughts.

Feelings of gratitude, love, hopefulness, joy, begin to raise the vibration and the energy you are sitting with into those of powerful, elevated positive emotions. The more time you spend in this elevated state, the more you are raising your consciousness and rewiring your brain toward calm, happiness, peace, prosperity and love. Just *by truly feeling into those moments,* you are connecting with your spiritual body and allowing it to expand—resetting and relaxing your mental and emotional bodies as you focus on positive feelings.

While you're in this space of possibility, embodying a higher level of emotion, there is less room to focus on the things that are missing, so you move away from the things *causing* you stress. As you do this, you are *rewiring your physical body back to calm.* This process alone connects all four bodies as you free yourself from worry. It's incredibly powerful. Later on, we will talk about how to incorporate bringing thoughts of abundance into your daily routine.

For now, just understand that your brain, nervous system, and all the biochemicals involved in that calm, rest-and-digest process all align to bring you back to calm. The more you do this, the more you strengthen your body's natural inclination to remain calm or return there quickly. The more time you spend thinking about how much you already have, you begin to rewire your brain to steer away from the negative and pay more attention to the positive. Dr. Rick Hanson, Neuropsychologist and author of the book *Hardwiring Happiness*, talks about the green zone and the red zone. The green zone refers to our calm state of rest-and-digest, whereas the red zone refers to fight-or-flight mode. He describes the following:

> "Green is the resting state, the home base, of the brain and body, characterized by activation of the parasympathetic nervous system, repair and refueling of bodily systems, and a peaceful, happy, and loving mind. In Green, we are usually benevolent toward ourselves, others, and the world.
>
> Then we rev up into Red in order to avoid threats, pursue opportunities, or deal with relationship issues: the sympathetic (fight-or-flight) nervous system activates, stress hormones like cortisol course through the bloodstream, and (broadly defined) hatred, greed, and heartache course through the mind. In Red, we're primed for fear, possessiveness, and aggression. If you're upset—if you're anxious, frustrated, irritated, or feeling put down or inadequate—you're in Red or heading there quickly.

In a busy life, each day gives you dozens of opportunities to leave the Red zone and move toward Green. Each time you do this, you gradually strengthen the neural substrates of Green, one synapse at a time."[40]

Taking time to focus on powerful positive emotions and thoughts—like love, abundance, happiness, peace and calm—is a practice that can retrain your brain to stay in the "green zone."

Shift Your Mindset

Once you cultivate a more abundant state of mind you will rapidly shift your mindset to one of possibility and ease. In order to shift to a new reality, we need to shift our mindset first. To help you do this, you need to be able to visualize it in a clear way. Get really specific on what it is you'd like to create for yourself. Visualize it *as though you've already achieved it*—think of a specific moment in time when you will have already accomplished it—imagine what you'd see, hear, and feel once you already have it. The more time you spend focusing on the abundance of what you want to create for yourself in your life—the more you stay in this calmer state and retrain your brain to strengthen these neural pathways. As you do this, you create a new reality because you've shifted your mindset to one of creation, abundance, happiness and success.

I had a client who was an artist who had trouble shifting her mindset. She had an upcoming meeting where she was going to present her art piece and the budget for the project to her customers. The meeting had her stressed out and feeling unsure about how to present the project.

She had a lot of resistance to the idea of the meeting going well. Her main concern was if the client would be appalled at the budget of this piece. She thought he'd say it was too expensive.

I asked her "How would you know he was thinking that?"

"Well, what if he makes a face when I tell him the cost of the project?" she said.

I suggested that in that case, she was making an assumption.

I asked, "What if you could make the face mean something different? What if you could tell yourself a different story? What if the face he made was another way of him saying, *Oh, my God, that's so much lower than anticipated! Absolutely, we can do that!*"

It was a small reframe of the conversation and then we created a quick visualization of her closing the deal. And now she is so excited to have built this incredible art installation in Miami.

Going Beyond What's Fathomable

"Imagination is more important than knowledge."

—Albert Einstein

Imagine yourself already having accomplished a goal. Then, imagine a crystal clear moment in that world—what are you doing? Are you standing on the beach? Are you unlocking the door to a brand new home you just purchased? Are you with your kids? What does that moment look like? Are you on a stage being celebrated and receiving an award? Are you being congratulated by your team?

After you see the accomplishment in your mind and hear it happening you begin to feel it in your body. As the image unfolds it begins to feel very real and a new neural pathway lights up. You start to have thoughts like—*Oh, my God, I can totally do this! And, I already have!* This is the process of rewiring the brain.

It's an easy process in some ways, but sometimes we need a little help to get beyond our blindspots. This reminds me of the work I did with a client we'll call David, who was about to publish his book. He came to me when he'd been inundated by all kinds of fears around whether the book would do well. I suggested that whenever he felt fear and doubt, to practice a pause.

Then, I coached him to allow himself to experience the joy of getting back into that moment of completing the book. I asked if he could reset and go back to that moment where he already pictured the completed book. But I also asked him to imagine some other moments that went beyond what he could fathom. Like when he held the book in his hand or saw it in the bookstores for the first time.

I wanted David to allow himself to have that joy overlap with a moment where he might imagine his publisher calling, saying, *David, I know you're on holiday right now but I wanted to let you know the great news! We just sold a million copies!* I asked him to imagine a bunch of other moments that he could string together (as unrealistic as they may have felt to him then) and coached him to suspend his disbelief and just go there, stringing the events together. Because the more moments you can imagine, the more you can string them together like a set of pearls, the more you hardwire that neurology, creating a visual for new possibilities, new habits, getting rid of fear, doubt and limitations. You're essentially hardwiring new thoughts, feelings and behaviors together that are far more empowering.

In the coaching world, for example, we want people to get a visual, auditory and kinesthetic representation as though they've already done it. Neuroscience research says, when you're visualizing, you're tapping into the visual processing, problem-solving, auditory and tactile processing areas of the brain. You're literally lighting up the visual, auditory and kinesthetic areas of the brain. If you want a powerful neurohack to supercharge your visualizations, make sure you have these covered.

When you do, you begin to create a world where you can step into a new reality because *the brain doesn't actually know if what you are envisioning is real or perceived.* If you can imagine a new reality, then you can create a new reality. If you can imagine yourself running that race, you can imagine winning. The first time somebody broke the 10-second record for the 100-meter dash, it was considered impossible. Then suddenly, one guy did it, and then a second guy, and then a third guy and now it's the new benchmark.

We've seen skiers use visualization to imagine every second of their race just before the actual race. Dr. Denis Waitley, author of The Psychology of Winning, and former chairman of the U.S. Olympic Committee Sports Medicine was hired to teach athletes the power of visualization or Visual Motor Rehearsal.

Here are the observations from Dr. Waitley—

Using this program, Olympic athletes ran their event—but only in their minds. They visualized how they looked and felt when they were actually participating in their event.

The athletes were then hooked up to a sophisticated biofeedback machine, and its results told the real story about the value of visualization. The neural transmitters that fired were the same that actually fired the muscles in the same sequence as when they were actually running on the track!

This proved that the mind can't tell the difference between whether you're really doing something or whether it's just a visual practice. Dr. Waitley says, "If you've been there in the mind you'll go there in the body."[41]

In a very real way, using visualization, you can begin to design a new reality, one that has you feeling empowered, certain, capable and victorious at whatever you can imagine.

Strengthen Your Intuition

When we are grounded in our values we align the universe to our needs and deepest desires. In a way, when we can name and claim them, it helps our intuition kick in like it never has before. Values are a kind of antenna that draws events and experiences to us. When we get clear about them, our intuition takes over and helps us navigate the world according to them. Think of our intuition like a kind of GPS that lets us know when we are about to take a wrong turn—not honoring our values.

We all have a sense of what intuition is but *do we really know*? People like to define intuition as a gut instinct. That ever-powerful first moment when you meet a new person or situation and you can sense if they are good or bad for you. It's the ability to understand a situation immediately, without the need for conscious reasoning. Intuition comes from an instinctive feeling rather than conscious thinking.

So if intuition is beyond consciousness, then is it *UN-conscious*?

In my study of neuroscience, I learned that we operate 5% in the conscious brain and 95% in the subconscious brain. Just take a moment and process that for a moment. 95% of how we experience our world occurs in our subconscious—beyond our awareness. So what if you could tap into the subconscious? What if you could learn how to communicate with it and reprogram yourself to be more resourceful? What if you could tune in to that 95% and gain real insight?

In the world of Neurolinguistic Programming, it's believed that your *Subconscious Mind **IS** your intuition.* Your intuition can quickly assess people or situations and lets you know if they feel good or bad. When you are in tune with your values, intuition can guide you well, if you pay attention.

We've all experienced the feeling of letting our intuition be our guide. Think of a time when you were conflicted about some decision and when you decided to go with your gut or with what felt right. Have you ever noticed that it always feels right to trust your intuition?

But sometimes it can be a bit confusing. When fear, for example, comes into play, intuition can feel like instinct – this may be a (fear-based) survival response. When this happens it's good practice to check-in. Here's a quick way to make sure intuition isn't instinct—

- Take a few deep breaths.
- Say to yourself, "I trust my intuition completely."
- Then ponder the choices you have before you.
- Sit quietly, close your eyes, breathe calmly, deeply think of the choices and think of the result you want to produce.
- Soon, a particular choice will float into your awareness. This choice is usually your intuition or subconscious brain guiding you in that moment because you've taken the time to tune in and listen.
- When you have a single way forward, just take a moment to double-check. Does that choice *feel right* if you were to move forward with it? Can you see the end result you want if you were to make that choice? If it comes through clearly, then you're doing a good job of tapping into your subconscious or your intuition.
- It may take a little practice, but soon enough, this process will come to you even when you're not consciously thinking of it. If the direction or choice feels right after checking in, then TRUST that everything will come together easily.

Your intuition will never steer you wrong. It has your back 100% of the time. The more you trust your intuition, the more you will spend time making the right choices and waste less time fretting in the negative space of doubt where fear could convince you to make the wrong choices. In effect, by strengthening and acting in alignment with your intuition, you are also strengthening the neurology that you're doing it well. You'll find your mindset shifting from one of questioning to one of certainty. With certainty comes less worry and doubt. That clarity weakens the stress response and heightens our ability to stay in rest-and-digest, so we can remain healthier and in a happier, calmer state of mind.

TOOL #1:
Define Your Top Five Values

We talked earlier about how values are what's important to you. They are the guiding principles for how you interact with people and situations when you're being your most authentic self. Just like needs, when we are not living in alignment with what we value most, how could we possibly be living our best life? In the workbook, you'll get to go deeper. For now, take some time to think about your Top Five Values. It doesn't matter if it's not a complete list right now or even the ultimate list. We are a work in progress, so just be okay with that. We will continue to refine throughout our lives.

Define your top five values, the permeating themes that you wish to include in every aspect of your life—from your relationships to your work, and how you wish to spend your time in between. If you can use these values as the cornerstone, then you'll have a solid foundation for a whole new life that is far more fulfilling for you.

TOOL #2:
Practice Focusing on the Outcome You Want

Instead of worrying about all the things that could go wrong in your plan or your goals, practice focusing on the outcome you want and how you will feel when you get there. If that feels too big, then you can break the goal up into micro-goals—smaller milestones that you can accomplish on your way. You can also focus on any known obstacles and imagine yourself overcoming those.

In my study of positive psychology, we learned that there are two types of visualization— Process Visualization and Outcome Visualization. Process visualization is where you allow yourself to imagine the steps along the way to achieving your outcome. Outcome Visualization is seeing yourself in that moment when you will have already achieved it. Use both of these tools as you imagine each of your new goals, aligned with your values, and conquering the challenges until you reach the end state you desire.

For example, I had a client named Rose, who'd tried countless diets and exercise programs without ever reaching her ideal weight within ten pounds. Rose was only ever focused on the end goal. This can sometimes create a cycle of fantasy and disappointment. In this case, it was more effective to break the big goal into smaller ones and have her visualize one day and one week at a time. We talked about her greatest pitfalls and obstacles along the way. We set some smaller goals during the process—like how she'd respond to her late-night cravings or setting a new goal each week that she felt more doable. Fifteen pounds lighter and finally feeling capable of achieving anything, she's now become a weight loss coach herself!

TOOL #3:
Use Visualization To Imagine This New Life

Using Visual Motor Rehearsal, begin to create new neurology and string together several moments *in each category of needs* so that you have the IDEAL scenario built in. Imagine specific moments as though you already have what you desire. What are you DOING? Are you turning the key to your new home? Are you having a joyful moment with your family? Are you standing on a sandy beach? Get a really clear V-A-K representation—Visual, Auditory, Kinesthetic. *What do you SEE? What do you HEAR*? *What do you FEEL* in that moment where you already have a new reality for love, health, prosperity, connection, happiness?

Week 5:
R = REPEAT & REWIRE

"Neurons that fire together, wire together."

—**Donald Hebb,** a Canadian neuropsychologist known for his work in the field of associative learning

This week you will learn the importance of taking on certain activities so you can rewire the brain for optimal health. You will learn how to rewire away from old negative thought and feeling patterns and move toward more powerful thoughts and feelings which will provide you long lasting happiness. This week, we will go beyond awareness and understanding and learn it's important to put the information of the first 4 weeks into action. *Happiness is an active process where we become aware of, and make choices toward a happier, healthier and more successful existence.*

Neurons That Fire Together, Wire Together

Great saying, but what does this really mean? ***Neurons that fire together, wire together*** means that habits are formed through repetition. The more you run a neural circuit in your brain, the stronger that circuit becomes. In order to break the power of that circuit, we actually need to replace old habits with new ones. Each time you connect a more positive neural circuit, you do away with old habits and install new habits that have you feeling better and living a better quality of life. Wouldn't it be great if making those connections also felt easy and effortless? Stick with me in this chapter to discover how the brain and mind work and how our very thoughts can create a more efficient pathway to a happier life.

Back in 1949, Donald Hebb used this quote to explain neuroplasticity. He wanted to remind us all that every sensation, thought, experience, and emotion triggers thousands of neurons within a neural network. When you repeat an experience, neurons are triggered each time by the brain. This can be good and bad. If you are focused on the negative or a mix of positive and negative, then we continue in that loop as we always have. So while we are thinking of wanting love and connection, we are also thinking how we don't have what we desire. The low vibrational feelings of not having love and connection continues to get hard wired within us, causing a perpetual state of *UN-happiness.*

Hebb's law basically states that nerve cells that fire together wire together. This demonstrates that if you repeatedly activate the same nerve cells (in the form of thoughts, feelings and behaviors), then each time they turn on it will be easier for them to fire in unison again. Eventually those neurons will develop a long term relationship.

> As Dr. Joe Dispenza says in his book, *Becoming Supernatural: How Common People Are Doing The Uncommon*,
>
> "Where Attention Goes, Energy Flows. Since where you place your attention is where you place your energy, when you wake up in the morning and immediately start putting your attention and energy on all the people you have to see that day, the places you have to go, the objects you own, and the things you have to do—your energy becomes fractured."

Consider, for a moment, that each of these people or things you give so much attention to is a known entity in your life because you've experienced it. You have a neurological network in your brain for each one of those people and things. Since they are mapped in your brain, you perceive and so experience them from your past. If how you think and how you feel determines the frequency and information you are emitting in your energy field—which has a significant effect on your life—and if all your attention (and so all your energy) is tied up in your outer world of people, objects, things, places and time, there is no energy left in your inner world of thoughts and feelings."[42]

He goes so far as to say that we actually become addicted to certain emotions and the stronger the addiction, the more attention we give to it. The only way to break this cycle of old thinking is to *install* new ways of thinking and feeling. This is a diligent practice, beginning with the start of each day and continuing throughout the day. It takes constantly focusing and refocusing your attention back to what you want to feel and think about. What you think about, you bring about. New thoughts and feelings together bring about a new state of being—*a desired state of being.*

Neurons wire together because the brain is designed to be efficient. The more frequently we do something, the more hardwired the brain becomes. Eventually, those frequent connections turn into the path of least resistance. In the whole discussion of building new and healthier habits, we can all agree that it plain old sucks that we can't just remove old unwanted habits.

In order to form new habits, we must create new habits or behaviors. As we perform new behaviors repeatedly, we memorize and hardwire new thoughts, feelings and behaviors together. Now bare with me here as I geek out on neuroscience a bit and provide a scientific explanation for this. Until the mid-1900's, neuroscientists believed the brain stopped growing at the age of 17 and then would be fixed or static throughout adulthood. Only in recent decades has it been discovered that the brain is dynamic and actually changes at a rapid rate. We are fully capable even of stimulating new neurons (neurogenesis) and creating lasting change in the brain (neuroplasticity).

As Dawson Church states in his book, *Mind over Matter*—

"Even the structure of neurons is constantly changing. Microtubules are the scaffolding that gives cells their rigidity, similar to a way that girders shape a building. The microtubules in the brain's nerve cells have a shelf life of *just ten minutes* between creation and destruction (Kim & Coulombe, 2010). That's how quickly our brains are changing. In this seething mass of activity, selected neural circuits are enhanced. *The ones that grow are the ones we use.* Pass an information signal repeatedly through a neural bundle and the bundle starts to enlarge. *Just as the arms of a bodybuilder get bigger as he practices lifting heavier weights, our neural circuits grow when we exercise them.*"[43]

If the brain's nerve cells have a shelf life of about ten minutes between creation and destruction, then willfully focusing on what we want to create and paying attention to just a new set of thoughts, feelings and behaviors is very powerful. If we are constantly cycling between what's new and what's stopping us, then we are allowing this process to unconsciously happen to us.

But if we take control back, just by being aware of the nature of this process, then we can remind ourselves to just stick with it and *keep resetting back to what we wish to create instead.* After some time, and some discomfort as we refocus our attention, this should get easier. As we repeatedly think, feel and act in a new set of ways, we will essentially *create a new shortcut to where we are going.* Great! Don't you just love the sound of that!?

Dawson Church also stated—

"...the speed of the process caused an earthquake in the world of scientific knowledge. When the neurons in a neural bundle are stimulated repeatedly, the number of synaptic connections *can double in just an hour*". If your house acted like your body, it would notice which lights you were turning on, and every hour it would double the amount of electrical conduit going to that light circuit.

To obtain the raw materials to rewire the rooms in which you turned on the lights the most, your smart home would strip wiring from other sources. Our bodies do the same. *Within three weeks of inactivity in an existing neural signaling pathway, the body starts to disassemble it in order to reuse those building blocks for active circuits (Kandel, 1998).*"

So think about it.... If you can just stick with it—resetting and refocusing for the first 3 weeks of our 6 week program—then it gets easier as the bonds between your old ways of thinking and feeling loosen their grip on you. We've talked about how we are constantly keeping ourselves in fight-or-flight mode. This research speaks to why it's critical to our happiness that we consistently hit the reset button and bring our attention back to a new way of being until it becomes unconscious.

If we *consciously* keep our thoughts, feelings and behaviors focused on the new, the desired and what we wish to create, then we can, over a period of just a few weeks, loosen the grip of old ways of being and put in place new ways that bring us greater satisfaction!

There are many ways to wire neurons together, here are some important concepts.

The Power Of Words

In Week 2 we talked about the Conscious Mind versus the Subconscious Mind. In the study of Neuroscience, we are taught that the conscious mind represents 5% of our thought processes and the subconscious mind represents the other 95%. So 95% of our thought processes are beyond our awareness!

When you study NLP, you also study Hypnotherapy, because there is a lot of overlap between the two studies of the subconscious. In fact, one of the keys to unlocking the power of the subconscious mind is understanding language patterns, the *L* or *Linguistics* part of NLP. Our very own inner dialogue and what we say to others or what we hear is taken as—this is BIG, so hold onto your seat—*a suggestion to the subconscious.* That's right. *Thoughts have that much power over us.* Everything we hear, feel or say gets absorbed into our subconscious and programmed into our bodies *like cellular memory.*

So if you're feeling or having a thought that you're not enough, or that you can't reach that goal or earn that money, then that thought and feeling pattern becomes wired as your new truth. If instead, you're telling yourself and feeling that you CAN do it, that you can have the love you deserve, have a life that excites you, earn that next milestone, be in the best shape of your life, then you're suggesting that to your subconscious and creating a new reality that follows.

The Power of Focused Thought Plus Positive Emotions

The HeartMath Institute did an interesting experiment on how the power of intentional thought and feeling together can manifest real physical change. HeartMath researchers have shown that physical aspects of DNA strands could be influenced by human intention plus elevated positive emotion. The article, *Modulation of DNA Conformation by Heart-Focused Intention* showed the following—

> "An individual holding three DNA samples was directed to generate heart coherence – an elevated state of mental, emotional and physical balance and harmony – with the aid of a HeartMath technique that utilizes heart breathing and intentional positive emotions. The subject succeeded, as directed, to intentionally and simultaneously unwind two of the DNA samples to different extents and leave the third unchanged. This was yet another example and real proof that the power of thought could alter our

physical reality. The results of the experiment showed evidence to support the hypothesis that our very DNA could be altered with intentionality. According to HeartMath, "Coherence is the state when the heart, mind and emotions are in energetic alignment and cooperation," HeartMath Institute Research Director Dr. Rollin McCraty says. ... This state is associated with sustained positive emotion and a high degree of mental and emotional stability."

In the DNA experiment, *individuals in a heart-focused, loving state are shown to be in a more coherent mode of physiological functioning and have a greater ability to alter the conformation of DNA.* "Individuals capable of generating high ratios of heart coherence were able to alter DNA conformation according to their intention. ... Control group participants showed low ratios of heart coherence and were unable to intentionally alter the conformation of DNA."[44]

Why Affirmations Work And Why They Don't

"Whether you believe it or not it's true"

— **Henry Ford**

Affirmations are positive statements that can help you overcome self-sabotage, negative thoughts, fear, and self-doubt. For affirmations to really work, though, it's not just a matter of saying the words. It's important to be able to embody them. In order to do this, you really need to be able to raise your vibration to that emotional state which you desire.

An example of an affirmation would be *I am a magnet for abundance and success*. The problem with just making the statement alone is that we usually also have thoughts of why we don't already have it. In effect, we are then sending out an inconsistent signal to the universe or energy field around us and so what we attract back to us is more proof of inconsistency.

You must really be able to *step into and embody* **only** the belief *I am already attracting abundance into my life in every way.*

If you can get into the feeling state of your affirmation, then you are vibrating at the level of the powerful emotions that go with that belief—I am certain, I am connected, I am prosperous and deserving. Just like the experiments conducted by the Heart Math Institute, its the *marriage of intention and positive emotions that create the coherence of your desires and reality.* It's this coherence that synchronizes with the universal field around us to create a new reality in line with our newly created balanced thought and feeling patterns.

The Secret Sauce to Manifestation

And there it is! The secret sauce to making affirmations work—also the secret sauce to empowering your visualizations and ultimately the formula to creating a new reality:

(Focused Thought or Intention)
+
(Positive Elevated Emotions for a sustained period)

= Increased Coherence in the four body system
= A New Reality

To simplify:

Intention + Elevated Emotion can alter the physical world around you. This is the trick to manifestation. Isn't that the outcome we are really trying to produce when we use affirmations or visualizations? An altered reality? One that has us feeling great, living a more inspired, meaningful and excited life, one that has us producing limitless results? Absolutely. Now you have the real power and you'll get to practice this with all the tools in your new arsenal in the workbook in Part III!

TOOL #1:
Set and Reset Your Intentions For The Day

"Everything in Life is Vibration"

– **Albert Einstein**

Take some time at the start of each day to focus on how you want to *feel*. You can begin simply by focusing on feeling peaceful, calm and happy. Really take time with each one, allowing the feelings and emotions to vibrate through you so that you completely embody them, until you feel you are in a completely new state of being. Then you can go outwards and think about the areas of your life. First focus on being in perfect health, then focus on your love life and family, your social community and how you want that to feel and look. Next, focus on seeing yourself achieving all of your goals will help strengthen the happy neural pathways you want and will help you to materialize your desires.

Start your day by focusing on how you want to *feel*, then how you imagine your day going so that it's just what you need. Imagine yourself feeling *happy, peaceful, calm, then imagine everything you need in your day coming together easily.*

If you begin the day with meditation, you can do this at the same time by focusing on what you'd like to create.

Sit with your coffee or just sit for five minutes at the start of the day and focus on very specific images of what you'd like to create in your life. *Always imagine.*

- *What will you see, hear and feel once you've accomplished your goal successfully?* Imagine several moments for each goal being accomplished.
- Imagine yourself in perfect health at any age

- Imagine specific moments in your relationships and how you want to feel
- Imagine your social and community life
- Imagine your work and career goals as you achieve them
- Imagine a life filled with meaning
- Imagine yourself feeling fulfilled

Whatever these moments look like for you, imagine yourself moving through the day and through each milestone with grace and ease, feeling completely loved, peaceful, and excited. As you visualize, include moments where your values are laced in. If you want freedom, then include moments where you feel free of worry and constraints or however that looks for you. Imagine yourself in each moment having endless options and the ability to choose whatever you desire.

You'll also find more energy in your day because you're wasting less energy with the things that used to worry you. You'll feel more productive, focused and relaxed, and begin your days and end your days in that coveted state of calm.

I used to wake up tired, stressing about the day ahead. Now I look forward to waking up, that smell of coffee and knowing I'm about to feel totally peaceful. It's a beautiful feeling to begin the day this way.

To make it even easier for you, I've carefully built this type of visualization into a guided meditation in the GetZend app (just go to www.getzend.com to download the app), where you'll find lots of ways to access healing, deep sleep, how to focus on goals, and a morning meditation too! We'll do more work on this morning mindset in the workbook in Part III.

TOOL #2:
The R.E.W.I.R.E. Triad™

After working with countless clients, I've spent years trying to find a way to counterbalance the effects of the five main limiting core beliefs and the years of programming that we now need to retrain to return to a mindset of love and abundance. Some of that old trauma requires deeper healing and may need you to do more inner work or get individual coaching.

Rebalancing the effects of the five main limiting core beliefs, though, is the first step to getting control over our old survival patterns and over those old thought and feeling loops that no longer serve you. If we can get ahead of the thoughts and feelings that would normally derail you and begin putting in place new thoughts and feelings, then you can begin wiring a new neurology that leaves you feeling more empowered. We are essentially laying the foundation for a new, healing, limitless version of you.

The R.E.W.I.R.E. Triad™ is the first step to how we overcome our limiting core beliefs. Again, here are the five most common limiting core beliefs.

- I'm Not Loved (or I'm Unworthy of Being Loved)
- I'm Undeserving of Wealth or Success or a Life I love
- I'm Alone (or Unsupported)
- I'm Not Safe (or not Protected)
- I'm Not (Good) Enough

The R.E.W.I.R.E. Triad™ consists of three groups of thoughts and feelings that begin to restore you back to wholeness. The R.E.W.I.R.E. Triad™ also includes a series of affirmations that shift your inner knowing back to feeling *certain, capable,* and *deserving.* As you go through each statement, I ask that you *feel into each statement.*

For example, when you say *I am certain that I am loved and fully supported in every way,* allow that feeling of love and support to vibrate through you. Repeat it over and over until you embody it with complete confidence. When you say, *I am capable of accomplishing my goals with ease and grace,* allow that feeling of ease to wash over you. When you say *I am deserving of the highest love and of all the abundance the universe has for me,* allow that to light you up totally.

Remember that the power of language—your language especially—is a suggestion to your subconscious mind. The more careful and intentional you are with your words, the more you are rewiring yourself for more love, greater connection, better health, more abundance, more meaning, and greater fulfillment. As you invite more compassionate and abundant words into your vocabulary, you will begin to create a new reality for yourself.

Feeling more *certain, capable, and deserving* is the foundation of how we can create change in our life. If we have a deep knowing that we are *certain, capable* and *deserving* of love in the highest form, of being in the optimal state of health, of being fully connected to God or source energy, of always being completely supported, then we are reprogramming away from fear and self-doubt. We are able to program away from survival mode and step into our own power and live life with happiness and purpose.

The R.E.W.I.R.E. Triad™ is about getting out of the old states of our being which yield the same results over time, leaving us with all the symptoms of not showing up in our lives—exhaustion, depression and depletion. Instead, we choose to embrace a new state of being where we are enough, where we are loved, supported, safe, and deserving of all the happiness and prosperity we can handle. Our new thoughts, feelings and behaviors build on each other and soon we are enjoying the experiences that fill us up and create more calm, peace and happiness in our lives. This new state of being brings new results.

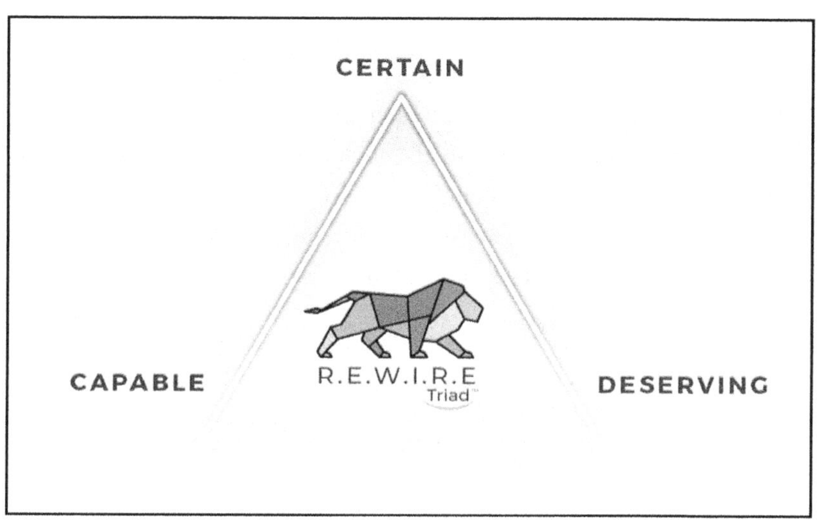

TOOL #3:
Commit To A Daily Practice

To repeat and rewire, we need a daily practice to begin to live our day from a state of calm. The easiest way to do this is to begin each day with a morning practice, in that deep knowing that you are safe, you are supported, you are loved and always looked after in the most abundant ways.

Find a few activities that allow you to begin your day in this new mindset and can keep you in this new state of being all day. For example, you can begin the day with a morning meditation to quiet your mind and bring the brain into coherence. You can use a guided meditation in the GetZENd app to guide you to a relaxed state and help you visualize a new outcome. Then, you can engage in activities that are aligned with your new desires. If you allow yourself to know that you are always being guided to make the right choices for you, then you begin to tap into your subconscious mind. This allows us to key into our intuition and make the kinds of choices that are in line with our values.

Essentially we need to be calm on demand. When you find yourself in a state of stress, you can actively return to a state of calm by practicing deep breathing. When it comes to effective maneuvers, any type of deep, slow diaphragm breathing—during which you visualize filling up the lower part of your lungs just above your belly button like a balloon, and then exhaling slowly—is going to stimulate your vagus nerve, which activates your parasympathetic nervous system, what controls your natural, calmer state.

Life happens, and events will trigger stress. This is a breathing technique you can use to quickly bring you back to balance. You can do this at any time to help you return to your natural state of rest-and-digest. When you feel stress coming on, take six deep breaths to re-engage the parasympathetic nervous system, which sends a signal to your brain to tell the anxious part that you're safe and you can return to your state of calm.

The more you breathe deeply, the more quickly you can go from feeling stressed to feeling relaxed. As you master this technique, you rewire your neurology to not only return to this calm state more quickly, but you will also find you spend more time there, leaving you in a better state of overall health, happiness, and in greater tune with your intuition so you can make decisions and choices that are in line with your core values.

Week 6:

E=ELEVATE & EXPAND

As we have discovered in previous chapters, we are actually wired to pay more attention to the negative than we are to the positive. We evolved to have a heightened sense of attention to the negative in the event of danger. Even when there is no danger present, we still do this in life. Have you ever noticed that you can have a great day—say you give an amazing presentation and you get ten compliments—but if you hear one criticism, you tend to fixate on that one negative comment and spend way more time thinking of that versus the positive?

Extend Positive Moments

Each time we focus on the negative, we trigger our state of stress. In order to balance this out, we need to actively light up our state of calm. Take more time to focus on the positive things that happen and all the emotions that come with those moments. Celebrate those moments and the feelings that go with them! Have you ever noticed how little time we spend focusing on those strong positive moments and how much time we waste and fret about the negative ones?

A way to break this negative cycle is to allow yourself not only to feel happy, excited, and proud of what you accomplished but really *extend those moments.* The more time you spend in these powerful positive emotional states, the more you rewire your brains for greater joy, fulfillment, and success. Relish your victories and all those delicious feelings that come with doing something well! When someone pays you a compliment or shines a light on you, don't just redirect and shift focus away! Allow yourself to let it in! Then, take as much time as you can throughout your day to focus on those emotions. From now on, when positive events happen, take a few extra moments to really feel the positive feelings that come with those events. Doing so will retrain your brain to stay in your state of calm.

Increase Your Daily Intake of Positive Emotions

Just like when we nourish our physical bodies and develop mindfulness over what we take in, we need to do the same for our mental and emotional bodies. If we evolved to be good at survival and we have a natural Negativity Bias, then we need to learn to counter these tendencies. So instead of spending time ruminating, worrying and focusing on what goes wrong in our lives, we strengthen and build our ability to let in the good feelings.

So where do we start? Beginning the day in a peaceful state of mind is a great start.

Next, allow yourself to feel a sense of awe by savoring good moments when they happen. Dr. Rick Hanson, author of the book *Hardwiring Happiness*, recommends this practice, saying, "Several times a day, take in the good by really savoring a positive experience for 10-20 seconds or more." He mentions we have a habit of rushing to the next good thing and that prevents the current good things from seeping into our soul.

Taking this pause will help you to really absorb the good in your life and retrain your brain with the experience of more powerful, elevated positive emotions. As we do this, we are strengthening our practice of savoring the good moments and allowing them to expand the time spent FEELING good. This leaves less time to focus on negativity. In a very real way, we are training away from negativity and toward happier emotions.

Gratitude

Another way you can strengthen your ability to stay in your state of calm is to practice gratitude. So take a few moments to be present and enjoy the ride. Is it a gorgeous day? Take a moment to enjoy that and be thankful for the little things as well—for example, the sun shining, the friends and family you have (as few or as many people in your life that are close to you), the roof over your head, the ability to afford to eat and do things many people can't.

Take a few moments in the day to write down five simple things you're grateful for. Soon you'll start to find joy and appreciate each and every day. As you do this, you are wiring your brain to strengthen your calm response. Scientific evidence shows that practicing gratitude actually boosts the norepinephrine and serotonin levels in your brain—these are your brain's happy transmitters!

And the practice of being grateful helps stabilize these levels, which is essentially what anti-depressants do! If that isn't enough to convince you, try this on—in my study of positive psychology, also known as the study of happiness, I noticed that the bestselling books had some common themes and one of them was practicing gratitude. I decided it was best to give it a try.

To be fair, this is not always easy to practice when it feels like life is going wrong. In those moments, we can stop and ask, *What am I meant to learn from this? If there is a lesson here, then I'm grateful it happened as I'm grateful for the lessons learned.* Love the people in your life and remember—we are all doing the best we can with the resources we have. We all have our own journey and the timing of that is different for each of us. Be kind and compassionate when someone around you is struggling, and try to stay focused on how YOU want to feel.

When things go wrong, be grateful for what the experience taught us, then let go and reset. Keep the learning and discard the rest. This is a valuable lesson when things go wrong with people in your life. Being grateful for the learning experience—even when it can sometimes happen in a painful way—and learning how to leave the drama behind is a powerful skill to learn.

Psychology Today posted an article, titled *The 7 Scientifically Proven Benefits of Gratitude* in April 2015 which stated, "Gratitude improves psychological health. Gratitude reduces a multitude of toxic emotions, from envy and resentment to frustration and regret. Robert Emmons, a leading gratitude researcher, has conducted multiple studies on the link between gratitude and well-being. His research confirms that gratitude effectively increases happiness and reduces depression."

Eckhart Tolle, best-selling author of *The Power of Now* and *A New Earth: Awakening to your Life's Purpose* says, "Acknowledging the good that you already have in your life is the foundation for all abundance."[45]

Author of *Cosmic Ordering Guide*, Stephen Richards, had the following to say, "Gratitude also opens your eyes to the limitless potential of the universe, while dissatisfaction closes your eyes to it."[46]

Through my work with many coaching clients over the years, I've observed that it was in the darkest hours that they incurred the most personal growth. Isn't it usually in those moments of suffering when we learn patience and find our inner strength? Whether it's a beautiful moment or a challenging one, life is a journey meant to uncover who we really are. Take time to appreciate all of it—the joy and sadness—as we get closer to who we're meant to be with each passing day. Take a moment to be grateful we're moving into a new space and can welcome new and wonderful things into our lives.

EXTEND the good moments by consciously savoring the emotions that come with the positive events in your life. As you do this, you shift your mindset from what you don't have to what you can create. At the same time, you strengthen your brain's ability to remain calm, happy, and satisfied.

Find Your Tribe

We all need support. As you evolve into a new lighter state of being, you will find that you attract more like-minded people into your circle. You might also notice that some older relationships are challenging. Give yourself some room to let it all unfold naturally. If you're committed to your new state of being, then it's helpful to surround yourself with support—more importantly, to surround yourself with the right type of support. You want to create space for people to welcome the new you and resonate with your new ways of thinking and feeling. You will naturally find your soul tribe and they will find you. As you radiate a new positive outlook, the world and people will respond to you in new and amazing ways. Enjoy the journey.

We are social creatures and wired for connection. Brené Brown, research professor in social work at the University of Houston, defines connection in this way—"its the energy that exists between people when they feel seen, heard, and valued; when they can give and receive without judgment; and when they derive sustenance and strength from the relationship."

Studies in longevity have shown the number one reason people live the longest is because they belong to a tribe and have a strong social community. Staying connected and having a community where we have a sense of belonging fulfills our social needs on the most fundamental levels. So don't isolate yourself if old friendships fall away. They may respond better to the old stressed version of you. Allow yourself the space for those relationships to evolve and allow new ones to enter into your life who support the you that you're becoming. Eventually, you'll find the right balance and you'll be able to enjoy time alone, and time with friends and family because you choose it. You'll start to feel more at ease, more emotionally resilient, and more present in everything you do. Take time to engage in social activities that give you a sense of community.

Go Bigger!

Now that you understand the power of visualization and can imagine yourself in a whole new life, I'd like to invite you to ask yourself—*What if it can be so much bigger, more loving, more exciting, more meaningful than I am even capable of fathoming right now?*

Now that we have weakened the hold that the old fear and self-doubt had over you, what else can you imagine for yourself? What if you asked the Universe or Source to just show you what's possible?

What if we opened you up, but you can still only see a small number of possibilities? Can you allow your consciousness to expand and say, *I welcome love and abundance in the most miraculous of ways?*

Can you practice allowing yourself to be amazed with every new day?

Thought As Energy

"If you wish to find the secrets of the universe, think in terms of energy, frequency, and vibration."

—Nikola Tesla

Let's get into some Quantum Physics.

Remember your grade school days when you first learned about magnets and magnetic fields? I'd like for you to imagine two magnets. If you sprinkle iron filings around them, you'll see a clear pattern as the filings map out the energy fields produced. The neurons in your brain work the same way—they produce an energy field. Those fields have the power to shape the matter around them, just as the magnets cause the iron filings to form symmetrical patterns.

Let's call this symmetry *coherence.* Coherence is created when there is balance. Bigger magnetic fields outside the body, such as the earth's gravitational force, have an impact on our bodies, just like bigger magnets. They can shift the pattern of your body's fields. They influence your brain and body, just as your body, in turn, has a smaller influence on those bigger fields.

So here's another explanation for how we interact with people and the world around us. We all understand direct contact with other people, like a hug, but there's indirect as well. Your body's electromagnetic field extends outward about five meters from the center of your body. When you are within five meters of another person, your energy field is being influenced by theirs and vice versa.

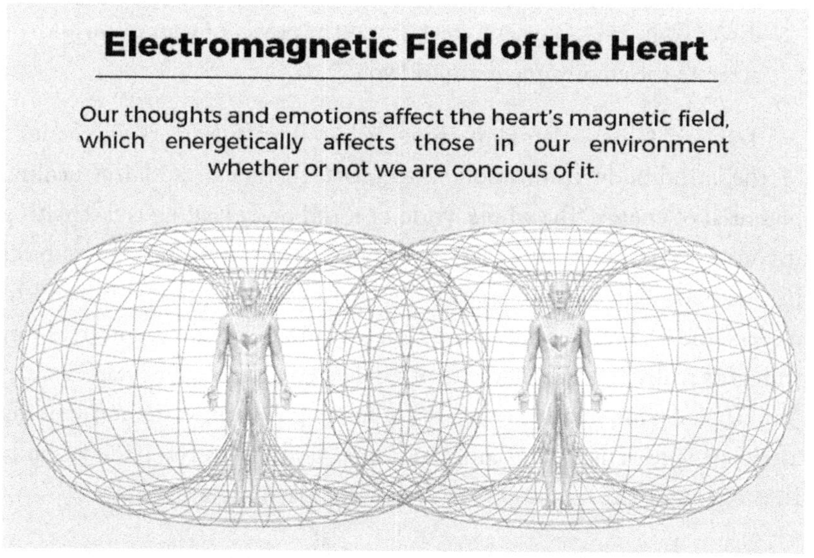

Think of a person you know who is happy and well-balanced, as compared to one that is more unstable. You can feel both energies. The well-balanced, coherent person feels like they flow better if we are in flow. The more unstable person might not flow with us as easily if we ourselves are in a relaxed and peaceful state of being. However, if agitated, this is definitely the right friend to call so that you can vent or commiserate.

Dr. Dawson Church, Author of *Mind to Matter, The Astonishing Science of How Your Brain Creates Material Reality*, and *The Genie In Your Genes*, has an interesting explanation for how thoughts interact with the universe around us—

> "When we originate an idea in consciousness, we send signals into the universal field. Transmission requires hardware, in the form of the brain, as well as software, in the form of the mind. Signals traveling through neural pathways create energy fields, and those fields change depending on the content of the consciousness.... Consciousness isn't something that simply is; it's something that can be controlled and pointed in a desired direction. When you direct your consciousness, you harness the power of your mind and activate the environment around you."[47]

Dawson Church has done some groundbreaking work in the area of the mind-body connection, integrative medicine, and the healing potential of energy. The whole world of mind-body healing is fascinating if you're interested in more. We will not get too deep into this subject in this book but we need to talk about it enough so that you begin to understand the interconnectedness of all things and how powerful our thoughts really are. When we are in a balanced and coherent state, we can produce amazing results in the area of healing. When we are not looking after our spiritual, mental and emotional bodies, it's the physical body that will show the symptoms, sometimes in alarming ways.

Here, I hope you'll indulge me and allow me to share a personal story. Back in 2008, I was diagnosed with vitiligo, a skin condition characterized by a lack of pigmentation in certain areas of the body. Well, as a sun worshipper, I can assure you, I was not happy at the prospect of avoiding the sun and didn't go out into the sun for a period of two years.

Anyone that knows me can tell you how much I love being out in the warm weather and feeling the sunshine on me. It's life-affirming!

After two years of hiding in the shade, I had a thought—*what if I could heal this?* As I sat there reflecting, I just asked the universe to assist me in finding some answers. I let my thoughts flow freely as if in a daydream. My first thought was *in nature, the most toxic animals, poisonous snakes or frogs, for example, all come with bright colors and stripes*, almost as nature's warning to us. I thought, *what if my vitiligo was my body's way of sending me a warning that something is wrong?*

I already knew when I'm not in alignment with who I am meant to be in this world that I do not feel well in some fashion. Perhaps it had been a while since I checked in with myself and examined the areas of my life to see if I was living my best life. I looked up vitiligo and realized it was classified as an autoimmune disease. Autoimmune is defined as a condition arising from an abnormal immune response to a functioning body part.

So my body was giving me a warning—I had large white spots on my olive skin. Next the autoimmune part meant that my otherwise healthy and functioning body was confused as to what was healthy and what was not—well if that's not a parallel for inner conflict, I don't know what is! Talk about an alarm bell going off! *What do I do now?*

That night as I laid in bed, I decided to have a dialog with my body. I began with awareness, thanking my body for showing up to support me and letting me know something was wrong. I reassured my body that I have other tools now and that I will begin to explore the areas of my life where there might be disharmony. Next, I lovingly said, *it's ok for you to heal now,* and I visualized all of those spots just filling back in with pigment. I kid you not, within two months, every single spot had filled in and there was no trace of any vitiligo on me. Thirteen years later, I'm happy to report, it never came back.

One of the other fears I had was if that condition was autoimmune, what would my body do next? I'm so glad that I saw the warnings early and did the work I needed to do to heal parts of my life where I was not living powerfully. It was a huge indicator to me that our physical bodies will serve and support us and even sometimes warn us when we have unhealed trauma. And this led me to discover how many ways we can heal our bodies, including harnessing our emotions.

Emotion As Vibration

"Everything is energy and that's all there is to it. Match the frequency of the reality you want and you cannot help but get that reality. It can be no other way. This is not philosophy. This is physics."

—Albert Einstein

There was a German physicist and musician named Ernst Chladni, who became interested in the study of sound and vibration. He was inspired by other scientists who made energy fields visible and developed a new device. When he placed fine sand on top of a horizontal metal plate, he ran a violin bow along the edge of the plate and caused the plate to vibrate. Afterward, he noticed that different vibrational frequencies produced different patterns in the sand. He became known as the father of acoustics and published his works, founding a new scientific field called Cymatics—the study of how sound or vibration affects matter.

According to Chladni, vibrations can change the configuration of material objects quite immediately. Water can also be made to change shape in response to different vibrations. Dr. Bernd Helmut Kroeplin conducted experiments at the Aerospace Institute in Stuttgart, Germany, measuring the effect of different people on water. A large group of students held a syringe filled with water and squeezed droplets of water onto a microscope slide. Kroeplin's team took photographs of the droplets. What they found was that each person's droplets were distinctly different from the droplets produced by others. The droplets produced by the same person, though, were virtually the same. They concluded that matter, in the form of water, passing through the energy field of a person produced an indelible and consistent impact on the matter.

Another study was performed at the Institute of Noetic Sciences in Petaluma, California. They were studying the effects of *distant intention* on water. A group of 2,000 people in Tokyo focused positive intentions on a batch of water samples in an electromagnetically-shielded room in Petaluma. The group of subjects in Tokyo were not aware that there were other control batches of water samples nearby. Photographs of ice crystals formed from both sets of water and were viewed by 100 independent judges. They discovered that water directed with positive intentions showed more beautiful and symmetrical shapes than the untreated water.[48]

Your body is 70 percent water. According to Dr. Dawson Church, water responds to vibrations around it as certainly as the sand particles on Chladni's plates or the water droplets in Kroeplin's microscope slides. He says "When you are flooding the water molecules of your body with the vibrations of healing energy, you are *entraining them in sympathy with wellness,* while discordant vibrations have the opposite effect. Immerse your mind in positive energy and at least 70 percent of the matter in your body comes into sync with that elevated state."[49]

How powerful is that?! We've all heard the saying "only good vibes" and now I get it. *We have the ability to choose* how we spend our time, who we spend it with and *how we want to think and feel at any given moment.*

And that brings us to a quote by Victor Frankl, "Everything can be taken from a man but one thing: the last of the human freedoms—to choose one's attitude in any given set of circumstances, to choose one's own way." Victor Frankl was a psychiatrist and Holocaust survivor, who wrote the book *Man's Search for Meaning*. In the book, he chronicles his experience but also brilliantly dissects human interaction in the most severe of circumstances. He described his psychotherapeutic method which involved defining a purpose in life, something to feel positive about, and immersively imagining a brighter outcome. Frankl positively correlated a prisoner's longevity with how positively he imagined the future.

Cultivating A Life Of Meaning

What is meaning and how is it different from purpose?

Meaning is now widely recognized as essential to human well-being, and numerous studies have documented the association between meaningfulness and a host of psychological benefits. In his book, *Meanings of Life*, Roy F. Baumeister argued that a meaningful life may be compatible with being unhappy, *but a happy life is impossible without meaning*. A sense of meaning supports happiness.[50]

In a Harvard report on measuring meaning, "Steger provides a thorough catalog of studies that have shown "people who believe their lives have meaning or purpose appear to be better off, including by being happier, enjoying greater overall well-being, and reporting higher life satisfaction, control over their lives, and work satisfaction. They also experience less negative affect and depression."[51]

So what's the difference between purpose and meaning? Some people use purpose and meaning interchangeably, but they are in fact different.[52] According to George and Park, "Meaning is a subjective experience of feeling that life fits into a larger context and has significance. It connotes a sense of comprehension and life as a whole makes sense."[53] Purpose, on the other hand, is defined as "an overall sense of goals and direction in life." George and Park concluded that *meaning contributes to greater emotional resilience*, the ability to bounce back after adversity.

> "Other People Matter. Period," said Dr. Chris Peterson, one of the founding fathers of positive psychology, when asked to define what positive psychology is.[54] He said, "I say that in every positive psychology lecture I give and every positive psychology workshop I conduct. It sounds like a bumper sticker slogan, but it's actually a good summary of what positive psychology research has shown about the good life broadly construed. It is in the company of others that we often experience pleasure and certainly how we best savor its aftermath. It is through character strengths that connect us to others—like gratitude—that many of us find satisfaction and meaning in life. It is with other people that we work, love, and play. Good relationships with other people may be a necessary condition for our own happiness, even in markedly individualist cultures like the contemporary United States."[55]

Cultivate Self Love

If other people matter and our relationships matter, then we also need to matter. We've talked about the necessity for healing past trauma and being able to arrive at a point where you can feel a sense of belonging here in this life, certainty that you are supported and loved, and deserving of respect and abundance in every way. The next step is to learn to be kinder to ourselves and turn that compassion inwards.

Kristin Neff is widely held as an expert in self-compassion. She defines self-compassion as being "kind and understanding when confronted with personal failings...It means that you act the same way toward yourself when you are going through a tough time that you would act towards a dear friend: noticing the suffering, **empathizing** or "suffering with" yourself, and offering kindness and understanding."[56]

> Dr. Deborah Koshaba states, "Self-love is not simply a state of feeling good. It is a state of appreciation for oneself that grows from actions that support our physical, psychological and spiritual growth. Self-love is dynamic; it grows through actions that mature us. When we act in ways that expand self-love in us, we begin to accept much better our weaknesses as well as our strengths, have less need to explain away our shortcomings, have compassion for ourselves as human beings struggling to find personal meaning, are more centered in our life purpose and values, and expect living fulfillment through our own efforts. It is about valuing yourself as a human being who is worthy of love and respect. If we can cultivate this more each day as we evolve, then we already begin feeling more at peace and can find that inner stillness that we all crave."[57]

TOOL #1:
Cultivate Self-Love

Some of the tools we have already discussed can be useful in learning how to cultivate a greater sense of self-love:

- **Mindfulness.** We have already learned to become the observer of our thoughts and feelings. People who have more self-love tend to know what they think, what they feel and what they want. They are more in tune with their own internal compass, their intuition, and will likely make life choices aligned with what makes them happy.
- **Learn to act on what you need, rather than what you want.** Sometimes what we want feeds the pleasure centers in our brain, but that pleasure is short-lived. If you act instead, based on

your needs, then you can make choices that keep you centered, grounded and moving forward in life. You can avoid the pitfalls of old patterns of behavior that get you stuck in a loop—like reaching for a glass of wine, or another glass of wine.

- **Set boundaries.** The people I've met in my career and in my life that get into the most trouble do not know how to set healthy boundaries. Stay true to your character, your values and say no to the things that don't resonate or that deplete you physically, emotionally, mentally and spiritually.
- **Protect yourself and your energy.** Be careful who you allow into your life. Make sure they are aligned with who you're becoming and want only the best for you. There will always be people that take advantage, that engage in negative activities and don't wish you or others well. If you're doing all this work to be your best self, then keep your circle smaller. Protect your energy fiercely.
- **Learn to forgive—yourself and others.** Practice being more merciful with yourself. Holding onto negative emotions can be so harmful to the physical body and can send the spiritual, mental, and emotional bodies into disharmony.

TOOL #2:
Meaning & Purpose

"Man's search for meaning is the primary motivation in his life and not a "secondary rationalization" of instinctual drives. This meaning is unique and specific in that it must and can be fulfilled by him alone; only then does it achieve a significance that will satisfy his own will to meaning."

—Victor Frankl, Austrian neurologist, psychiatrist, philosopher, author, and Holocaust survivor

Carin Rockind, my own professor of Applied Positive Psychology stated "Frankl (1963) suggested that we each have a uniqueness that is irreplaceable. Just as no two people have the same set of fingerprints, no two people have exactly the same set of strengths, talents, passions and experiences. Therefore, each person can make a distinct contribution to this world. Each of us has a unique purpose for our lives. People who live their purpose enjoy greater health, life satisfaction and overall well-being."[58 59]

Here's the fun part, just like needs and just like values, it's not a one-size-fits-all answer. What gives you meaning will be different than what gives someone else meaning. What I love about each of these concepts is that we are finding more and more that we are each unique and special in our own ways and that our role in this life is specific to our particular talents and passions. How great is that!?

If you don't yet know what gives your life meaning and purpose, that's fine. A good way to start is to look at the times in your life when you felt happiest or really connected. If you can find a way to use your natural strengths and talents and combine them with activities or causes you feel passionate about, then you are well on your way to understanding your unique purpose. If you are aligned with that, then you are living a life that truly lights you up.

For example, I've always been good at understanding complex concepts quickly. My top strength is that I am a strategic thinker. I can see patterns in large groups of data or people or projects. This served me very well in my first career as a management consultant. I added structure where there was disorder, I educated where knowledge was needed and strived to leave an organization equipped with new tools to be more successful. This also played out in my career as a success coach.

I also have a passion for helping and teaching others. Another passion is I'm a warrior for injustice. How could I not be, coming from South Africa? So it's natural that I am devoting my life to the study of multiple fields, many different modalities and that I use all of that knowledge to provide simpler guidelines while educating groups of people to find ways of improving the quality of their lives and raise their overall vibration. I work with at-risk girls and various non-profits where I teach emotional resilience, how the brain works, and how to rewire ourselves to be more fearless.

Use this as a guideline to start thinking about what your particular strengths and talents are. Think about the praise you get and what specifically moved or touched people in your interactions. In the workbook, you'll have a chance to map this out in more detail. But for now, just allow yourself to feel that deep knowing that you matter, that you belong and that the greatest gift you can bring to the world is YOU.

TOOL #3: Keep Your Vibration High

Be consistent with your thoughts. Be consistent with your emotions. Be consistent with where you focus your attention. If you feel yourself slipping into old ways of thinking and feeling, simply PAUSE & RESET TO KEEP YOUR VIBRATION HIGH.

As with the water experiments and Chladni's study of vibrations, our bodies respond to the vibrations we are exposed to, whether high or low.

Kroeplin stated "When you are flooding the water molecules of your body with the vibrations of healing energy, you are entraining them in sympathy with wellness, while discordant vibrations have the opposite effect. Immerse your mind in positive energy and at least 70 percent of the matter in your body comes into sync with that elevated state."[60]

Go Bigger. Allow yourself to just expand your possibilities, expand your consciousness and imagine a life so elevated that you feel as though you're living a dream.

If we focus our attention on remaining in an elevated state with positive emotions and thoughts, and we focus on our new outcomes, then you will find yourself feeling lighter, happier and living life with more ease.

It was my intention with this book to leave you with a roadmap of simple tools and an understanding of the research that demonstrates their benefits, with the hope that you will understand we are all in this together. It's time for us to go deeper and time for us to heal. I hope that this book and the following workbook will light the path for you to live your best life ever. I am leaving you with one of my favorite quotes which has been my guiding light for many years.

Our Deepest Fear

by Marianne Williamson

from *A Return To Love*

Our deepest fear is not that we are inadequate. Our deepest fear is that we are powerful beyond measure. It is our light, not our darkness that most frightens us. We ask ourselves, Who am I to be brilliant, gorgeous, talented, fabulous? Actually, who are you not to be? You are a child of God. Your playing small does not serve the world. There is nothing enlightened about shrinking so that other people won't feel insecure around you. We are all meant to shine, as children do. We were born to make manifest the glory of God that is within us. It's not just in some of us; it's in everyone. And as we let our own light shine, we unconsciously give other people permission to do the same. As we are liberated from our own fear, our presence automatically liberates others."

PART III:

THE R.E.W.I.R.E. SYSTEM™ WORKBOOK

Your How-To Guide for Reducing Stress, Developing Emotional Resilience & Maximizing Your Energy So You Can Be Happier

Welcome to Part III of the *6 Weeks to Happy* experience. By now, you should have all the tools you need to live a happier, more joyful and centered life. Follow this plan to continue to implement healthier habits while building and deepening new neural pathways as you transform your life and begin living with a renewed sense of calm and ease.

Since all happiness quizzes are self-rated, I've included one here for you to use with the indicators we've discussed throughout the book. This will act as a gauge so you can see how you are doing from week to week. I suggest beginning with a self-assessment at the start of the six-week program and do it again at the end of each week to chart your progress as you go. As you shift the needle in each area, you'll begin to see real change in your life. As the quality of your sleep improves and you hold less tension in your body, you'll find you are better able to regulate your energy, your mood, and your emotions.

After six weeks of completing these exercises, you'll have more tools to cultivate happiness. You'll spend less time in a state of stress, become healthier and better able to return to your state of calm quickly and easily.

The R.E.W.I.R.E. System™

Let's recap the R.E.W.I.R.E. System™. This program was designed to help you rewire your brain and reset your life so that you can be happier in just six weeks. Using a range of tools from neuroscience, Neuro-Linguistic Programming (NLP), psychology, mindfulness, positive psychology and others, this method will help shift your life in ways that leave you feeling lighter, less stressed, more vibrant and will help you move through your life with grace and ease.

Congratulations! These are the weeks that you've completed. After reading these summaries we will dive into in-depth exercises that will take your happiness to the next level.

Week 1: R=RELAX and Learn to Quiet the Mind

Using mindfulness and meditation, you'll develop greater self-awareness and begin to restore and strengthen your more natural, calmer state and weaken your response to stress.

Week 2: E=ELIMINATE the Noise

Simplify your life so that you spend your time and energy more wisely, more aligned with what you really want in your life.

Week 3: W=WHAT Do You Need?

What do you need so that you are happier in all areas of your life? This module is about examining your needs in a whole new way and redefining your life so that you can have those needs met and really feel as though you are thriving! As you do this you will also notice you are shifting your mindset so that you can create more of what you want in your life.

Week 4: I=IMAGINE & Visualize

This module is about developing a deeper sense of self-awareness so you have more clarity about what is working well for you and discarding what is not. Once you start to develop a clearer image of what you want to create in your life and how you want to feel, then the real fun begins. You get to become the architect and design a life you truly love! Once you know what that looks like, you can begin taking action and retrain your brain to your new life choices. As you do this, you hardwire a new mindset so that your reality aligns too.

Week 5: R=REPEAT & Rewire

"Neurons that fire together, wire together." By finding the right formula for you, you get to make this a daily practice, so that you put in place a new set of thoughts, feelings and actions that lead you into a more fulfilling life. This equips you with a set of tools to stay in that state of flow and gives you the ability to reset, repeat and rewire. Create a plan that can be repeated over six weeks to rewire your brain and your life for greater everything!

Week 6: E=ELEVATE & Expand

Elevating and expanding the good moments helps retrain the brain to stay in a calmer space, where you can finally feel like everything is going well. Part of rewiring the brain away from fight-or-flight and more toward our calmer state, rest-and-digest, means including the practice of consciously savoring the positive moments. If we are more inclined to pay attention to danger and negative situations, then we need to balance this out by choosing to spend more time on the positive moments. We need to celebrate life more and by allowing those good moments to extend we begin to hardwire our calmer, more natural state. In effect, we are learning to weaken our stress response, strengthen our calm response and allow more balance, and more emotional resilience.

As we go through each method, I will highlight which of the four bodies are affected—Spiritual, Mental, Emotional and Physical. Some tools will impact one or more of the bodies and some will also have secondary effects that affect the other bodies.

Let's begin with your first self-assessment.

The 6 Weeks to Happy Assessment

1. SLEEP QUALITY: 1☐ 2☐ 3☐
   Rate the quality of your sleep from 1 to 3, where 1 is Fair (less than 4 hours per night), 2 is Good (4 to 6 hours per night) and 3 is Great (7 or more hours per night)

2. TENSION IN THE BODY
   1☐ 2☐ 3☐
   Rate your level of tension in the body from 1 to 3, where 1 is Fair (breathing is labored, muscles are tight and tense in the neck and shoulders), 2 is Good (breathing is good, some tension in the neck and shoulders) and 3 is Great (breathing is relaxed and the body is no longer holding onto too much stress related tension)

3. ABILITY TO MANAGE ENERGY:
   1☐ 2☐ 3☐
   Rate your ability to manage and regulate your energy levels throughout the week, where 1 is Fair (very tired, not enough time and energy to do everything you need), 2 is Good (a bit tired, but getting better at prioritizing and managing your energy balance) and 3 is Great (sometimes tired, and overall doing well at re-prioritizing and making time to recharge)

4. ABILITY TO REGULATE MOOD & EMOTIONS:
   1☐ 2☐ 3☐
   Rate your ability to regulate your mood and emotions from 1 to 3, where 1 is Fair (irritable or easily agitated, short-tempered), 2 is Good (sometimes irritable or agitated), 3 is Great (able to choose your reactions more and stay calm)

5. STRESS LEVEL: 1☐ 2☐ 3☐
   Rate your stress level from 1 to 3, where 1 is Fair (moderate levels of worry, anxiety throughout the day), 2 is Good (low levels of worry and anxiety) and 3 is Great (knowing all is well and you're coping well)

6. FEELINGS OF HAPPINESS: 1☐ 2☐ 3☐
   Rate your feelings of happiness from 1 to 3, where 1 is Fair (infrequent feelings of hope, love, gratitude, joy, peace mixed with anxiety and worry), 2 is Good (frequent feelings of hope, love, gratitude, joy, peace) and 3 is Great (spending most of the day with feelings of happiness and a sense of grace and ease)

Week 1:
R = RELAX AND QUIET THE MIND

TOOL #1: Practice Mindfulness

Primary Intervention for Mental & Emotional Bodies

Secondary bodies affected: Spiritual / Energetic & Physical Bodies

> *"The quality or state of being conscious or aware of something. It's a mental state achieved by focusing one's awareness on the present moment, while calmly acknowledging and accepting one's feelings, thoughts, and bodily sensations, used as a therapeutic technique."*
>
> —The Oxford dictionary definition of *mindfulness*

Learning how to practice mindfulness feels a bit like time is slowing down, giving you time to just breathe, pause, and observe yourself. Rather than a constant jog on the hamster wheel of emotions and experiences, we get to step down off of it, practice the pause, and just be aware of how we respond. Being mindful is when you essentially *become the observer* of your life.

Imagine your breath, your walk, your thoughts and feelings. Sometimes, we believe we think or feel, as though they are conscious choices. But, unless we are actively engaged in conscious thought or conscious feeling, then we are simply *having thoughts* flow through us and the associated feelings as we engage with life. Quite literally your subconscious runs on autopilot as you go through your day if you let it.

For example, when you wake up, you start automatically having thoughts of how your body feels, or what you need to do that day. As you have thoughts about your day, specific feelings may come up—fatigue, worry, stress, excitement, nervousness among others. Now imagine, if you can, a practice of observing yourself more. *This creates some distance between the things worrying you and the you doing the worrying.* To do this, picture yourself sitting there, drinking your coffee. Instead of worrying about your day, just observe yourself having worrisome thoughts.

It's a bit like watching yourself through a window. By putting some distance between you and the subconscious thoughts and feelings, you create a new level of heightened awareness. You become increasingly aware of your thoughts and emotions and over a fairly short period of time, you will start to notice the patterns. You will start to notice which thoughts and feelings have woven together and you also start noticing why. As you practice being mindful, you'll start to see why and when you get frustrated, or when self-doubt creeps in, or when you feel hurt or triggered.

You'll start to notice patterns in how your energy flows too, who you're with, what you're doing, when you're eating or drinking or socializing or resting or when you're resisting things. You will begin to develop a deeper sense of self-awareness. *With awareness comes the ability to pause.* Because you are not completely in the events, you are observing yourself in the events. It's as if time itself has slowed down, and you can take an extra breath, you can pause before reacting, or pause after reacting and *just notice.* The more awareness you develop, the more you get to be in control of your emotions, your thoughts, your energy, and ultimately your choices.

There's no right way to do this and no wrong way. Mindfulness can be practiced in a variety of ways. For now, just start by noticing and observing yourself as you wake up, throughout the day and as you finish the day.

There are two simple steps:

1. Just observe without judgment.
2. Practice the Pause.

Over time, you'll notice you have greater insight, you will have developed a much stronger relationship with your intuition, you'll be more in control of your emotions, more relaxed and yet more focused. That's it. It's that simple. Just observe. And Practice the Pause.

"Feel the feeling, but don't become the emotion. Witness it. Allow it. Release it."

—**Crystal Andrus Morissette,** worldwide leader in the field of self-discovery and personal transformation

TOOL #2:

Identify Your Limiting Core Beliefs & Rewrite Your Story

Primary Intervention for Mental & Emotional Bodies

Secondary Bodies affected: Spiritual / Energetic & Physical Bodies

This is where we get to go deeper and heal the unhealed parts of ourselves that are craving stability, love, nourishment and an invitation back to wholeness. We have all suffered childhood trauma, adolescent challenges, and painful experiences that have shaped who we are and how we interact with the world. The time has come for us to heal. It's no accident that you're reading this passage. As you do this, it allows for reconnection and deepening of the connection with your spiritual or energetic body and with source energy.

The inner you, the subconscious you, the energetic you, have been calling you to do this for some time. If little things still trigger you from time to time—whether it's in small ways or big ways—then it's time for action. It's time to let the past go and cultivate a deeper understanding of ourselves and a sense of self-love and compassion that wasn't possible before. When you have that, you can stop looking for it in other people, in achievements, in things, and bring yourself back to balance.

Remember, if we choose not to heal, or don't realize we need to be healed, we will continually get triggered and be presented with opportunities to heal. These opportunities present themselves as tricky situations, people that hurt or disappoint us, relationship issues, financial struggles, health issues and failed attempts at happiness and prosperity.

As we go through this journey called life, we are meant to evolve in order to find greater peace, better health, more balance, more joy, gratitude and meaning. If you're wishing for more peace in your life, it doesn't magically appear. You normally get presented with a number of challenges until you do your healing. You get to discover the parts of you that need healing, and then you have to do the work to heal in order to find peace. The cycle will repeat over and over until we heal. Furthermore, if the mental and emotional bodies are not healed, this will likely result in your physical body calling for your attention by way of injury, chronic pain, inflammation, disease and illness.

The early trauma that occurs usually leaves us with a set of limiting core beliefs. This is where most of our self-doubt comes from, and forms our sense of trust or lack of trust in relationships—like fear of abandonment, and feelings of not being worthy.

In this next section, we will go over the Five Main Limiting Core Beliefs that are common to most people. We will take a look at how it may show up in your life and where it may be limiting you from having the loving, fulfilling relationships you desire or from having a deep sense of joy and belonging to the life you have now. Lastly, we will look at ways you can change the narrative dictated by your limiting core beliefs.

Freeing Yourself From Your Limiting Core Beliefs

Please take note of each of the limiting core beliefs, and also take note of how they may be affecting you in different areas of your life. You may or may not hold all five of these beliefs. Some people have two or three core beliefs that are disruptive. If you can discover those, then they unlock any emotions trapped by them too. You will also notice that some of the behavioral patterns or strategies are similar. That's okay, they were built for survival, and so were you. But it's time for us to leave survival mode and move toward happiness.

Once again, here are the Five Main Limiting Core Beliefs:

- I'm Not Loved (or I'm Unworthy of Being Loved)
- I'm Undeserving of Wealth or Success or a Life I Love
- I'm Alone (or Unsupported)
- I'm Not Safe (or not Protected)
- I'm Not (Good) Enough

Step 1:

For the Limiting Core Beliefs you may have, we need to uncover the precise wording that feels most appropriate for you, in order to unlock the hold it has on you. We already spoke about the power of words, so the specific language pattern is key. For each limiting core belief, I'll provide a few examples of the wording.

For each example, just take a few deep breaths, open a dialogue with your subconscious, and ask yourself, *"When did you decide that...*You're not loved?" for example. If the wording is the right language pattern for you, you will feel it immediately. The part of you that needs healing will feel a well of emotions when you hit the right phrase—sadness, loneliness, disappointment. If it's not the right wording, you won't feel it as strongly.

It is important to sit with each phrase and just observe how you feel. When you find the right phrase—that's what will need healing within... and so it begins. This is the most loving and compassionate thing you can do for yourself and is the most powerful step you can take toward real self-love and true happiness.

Step 2:

Each of these Limiting Core Beliefs comes with a set of negative emotions and patterns of behaviors that are linked together. If you can identify them, you can start to unravel them and the hold they have over your subconscious now, so that you will have more choice over how you respond to people and events in your life. I've listed some common patterns of behavior—let's call these subconscious strategies—that are ways these beliefs can play out in your life. Your particular set of strategies may not be exactly like each one here but will be similar enough that you can see the patterns yourself. So take note of whether each strategy is applicable to you and how it shows up in your behavior.

We will use the first one as an example—I'm not Loved.

Lastly, we get to dismantle these beliefs and begin to pull these pieces back into wholeness, forming a healthier narrative, and bring ourselves back to love.

Step 3:

In order to heal from this belief, we need to find evidence in our lives to disprove it. Our subconscious likes to look for things to support our beliefs—the belief then becomes a self-fulfilling prophecy. How weird and wonderful our subconscious is! And also, how exhausting. Are you done with that old pattern of self-sabotage? Let's say, YES! It's time to move forward and leave doubt and shame in the dust.

On to the fun part! Instead of looking for things to support this belief, we need to identify evidence to the contrary. What is your evidence procedure? In other words, for our example, ask, *How will I know when I AM LOVED?* This is when you get to REWRITE YOUR STORY. Your limiting core beliefs don't have to be your life story.

We have over 2 million bits of information per second around us at any moment, (the scenery around us, the lighting, shadows, sounds, conversations, thoughts, feelings, etc.) but the conscious mind can only process around 7 chunks of information per second, or 134 bits per second. So what do we do with the rest? We delete, distort and generalize. Remember, the brain is designed to be efficient. Essentially, we quickly judge the event, add meaning, categorize it and file it away as memory.

But if our interpretation wasn't 100% of the full picture, then how could it be 100% true? If it's not true, then it doesn't have to be our truth. It's only one of a countless number of possibilities. If we created this belief from an incomplete set of data, then we can easily disprove it and reclaim our lives. We can change our story so that we feel more connected, more fulfilled, more loved, more deserving, more alive.

So let's get started.

I'm Not Loved

Step 1: Identify the language pattern that resonates most deeply for you

Most Common Variations on the wording

- I'm not loveable
- I'm not deserving of love
- I don't deserve love
- I'm not worthy of real love
- I'm not easy to love

- I'm not loved
- I'm unworthy of being loved

Step 2: Identify your subconscious strategies that relate to this belief

(Subconscious strategies are patterns of behavior toward an overall goal)

- Short term relationships (less than five years), especially past the mid-life point
- Pushing people away, solitary behavior when you wish to connect instead
- Leaving or ending relationships when they feel too challenging
- Allowing others to dictate who or how you should love
- Needing lots of attention or validation from others, inappropriate flirting or over the top behavior just to see if you can win someone's affection or attention
- Lack of healthy boundaries with friends and partners
- Codependent and/or controlling relationships; need to control your partner and relationships
- Lack of trust and/or fear of abandonment
- Feeling unimportant or insignificant in relationships, even when there is plenty of evidence to the contrary

Step 3: Find examples of evidence to rewrite your story

Remember your Love Language here as well as how this plays into what makes you feel loved. Sometimes your loved one shows you they love you in ways you don't realize. Sometimes we get mixed messages. If you're only looking for evidence to support that you are not loved, then that's all you will see. If you allow yourself to see the rest of the evidence, you could actually find that you are loved and that the people in your life are showing you in lots of ways. However, because of the limiting belief you used to hold, you couldn't see it, and now you can. If you've uncovered the underlying belief, then you can see more clearly when love is demonstrated and allow it in so that you KNOW THAT YOU ARE LOVED.

- Your partner or loved one makes an effort to make you feel special or appreciated in some way
- Words of love, affection and adoration. Words of praise or appreciation.
- Physical affection, touch
- Gestures of love—going out of their way to make your life easier or to support you in some way
- Gifts or tokens of appreciation, a surprise to show you they care
- Even in tough times, they still *try*
- Spending quality time together, planning activities together, making time for you
- Making any effort, in the ways they are able to

I'm Undeserving of Wealth, Abundance, Success

Step 1: Identify the language pattern that resonates most deeply for you

Most Common Variations on the wording:

- I don't deserve that amount of wealth
- I'm not deserving of that much success
- I don't need that much
- I'm not lucky enough to be that successful
- That type of wealth is impossible for most people
- Wealth or abundance is just a dream
- I'll never be able to achieve that
- I'll never amount to much
- I don't have the education or experience I need to be successful
- My life and my work doesn't require more

- I'm happy with what I have (this sounds positive and it may be a statement of contentment for some. For others, it could be a limiting belief, so just try it on and see)

Step 2: Identify your subconscious strategies that relate to this belief

- Creating wealth and then losing it
- Not having a financial plan so that you can accumulate wealth
- Lack of planning for the future, spending as quickly as you earn
- Spending beyond your means
- Believing that struggle is the meaning of life, money doesn't grow on trees, money is the root of all evil, (any related expression that suppresses your ability to create abundance)
- Being miserly, lacking joy when spending money to enjoy life or pleasure
- Never really going after your goals to completion
- Starting and quitting different ventures, preventing yourself from being resourceful
- Surrounding yourself with people with a similar relationship to money, success or prosperity (keeping you stuck)
- Discomfort around successful people
- Social comparison to those with more, envy and/or negative thoughts about those with more
- Fear of Failure / Fear of Success

Step 3: Find examples of evidence to rewrite your story

Try to think of all of the things in your life that made you nervous, like starting your first job and wondering if you could do it well, or having a child. Think of the moments where life could not have prepared you for the task when it arrived, but you stood up, got it done and learned how to do it well!

This is where you get to prove to yourself that even when you thought you couldn't, you did! You figured out how to do it. And if you can do that, then you can do something new. Think of all the money you've already earned, how much abundance you've already experienced and remember that YOU ARE DESERVING OF SUCCESS in every way.

Remember also that your subconscious has created a story about money, about having it or not having it, about your ability to create it or whether or not you deserve to have it in your life. You created a story about the life you deserve to live and how much pleasure and enjoyment you get to have. You also likely created a story about how stressed or worried you should be about finances. I know many spiritual people who believe that to be of service means they shouldn't be making too much money, and so they're always fighting to pay bills. Who says so? When did you decide that to be of service meant you had to live in scarcity?

If the universe is so abundant, then surely there's enough for everyone to have what they need and to enjoy life's pleasures along the way. Isn't it true that if you are a person dedicating your life to helping others, then you could do more good if you had more? Chances are if your parents or family members or social circle had views like *success means you have to struggle*, then those beliefs probably became yours. Their living in scarcity was felt by you as a child and so, even later in life, when you are successful, it may feel to you like you are still constantly in a state of worry. Remember that we are reprogramming *away from survival here* and moving *toward hope and prosperity.* In order to get there, we need to uncover why you're stuck in an old way of thinking. So *what are your survival-based beliefs around money* or success or abundance?

If you've uncovered the underlying beliefs, then you can see more clearly when success does flow towards you and you can welcome it in, *KNOWING THAT YOU ARE DESERVING.* Here is how you can notice some evidence to the contrary:

- Calculate how much you already have earned over the years. You might likely be shocked to see how much wealth you already have acquired

- Notice how many opportunities presented themselves to create more abundance
- Notice all the blessings in your life already and how much you can be grateful for
- Redefine what success means to you and note how you already have it
- Notice how many times you thought you couldn't but you DID, so YES YOU CAN
- Notice where in your life you did accomplish a lot. If you did it before, you can do it again
- Notice how much you've acquired when you believed you didn't deserve it
- Imagine how much more abundance you can have now that YOU KNOW YOU DESERVE IT

I'm Alone (or Unsupported)

Step 1: Identify the language pattern that resonates most deeply for you

Most Common Variations on the wording:

- I can only rely on myself, I can't depend on anyone but myself
- No one's ever really been there for me
- I don't need anyone, I don't need anyone to look after me
- It's hard for me to ask for help, I like to do things on my own
- I don't have any real support
- I'm more of a loner, I like to keep to myself
- Disconnection from Source, God / I don't believe in God or Energy

Step 2: Identify your subconscious strategies that relate to this belief

- Lack of Trust in people and relationships
- Highly independent, autonomous but tending towards unhealthy limits
- Short lived relationships
- Inability to find a suitable partner
- Frustration working or cooperating with others
- Keeping people at arm's length, never really letting anyone get close to you
- Loss of faith in God, Source, the Universe

Step 3: Find examples of evidence to rewrite your story

Notice how family and friends are there to support you, or, notice how they were there before you disconnected

- Note how, even in the dark times, there was a lesson or an inner voice guiding you to make the right choice
- Go back to when you last disconnected from someone you love and imagine a new outcome where you are supported and surrounded with love
- Notice how every time something unexpected happened, it ended up being for your highest good
- Start a dialogue with God / the Universe and ask for messages to help you find your peace, then listen and notice. The answers are everywhere if you are open
- Reconnect with a loved one and allow yourself to ask for support, notice how they are there for you and how much they want to be there for you

I'm Not Safe (I'm not Protected)

Step 1: Identify the language pattern that resonates most deeply for you

Most Common Variations on the wording:

- I'm not safe
- I don't feel secure; I've never had security
- No one is around to protect me
- It's normal to always worry or be anxious
- I always feel a bit unstable, like everything good could disappear in a moment
- I always need to protect myself

Step 2: Identify your subconscious strategies that relate to this belief

Pushing people away, not allowing anyone to get too close

- Lack or Fear of Commitment
- Always worrying about money
- Tendency to question your partnership; Always wondering if there is a better partner
- Avoidance behavior to numb emotions - overconsumption of food, alcohol, medications, even social and other distractions like compulsive shopping
- Need for constant company or attention
- Lack of willingness to work through old trauma (this has been your safety net for so long, that there is fear in letting that go, even though the rewards of letting this go are so much greater)

Step 3: Find Examples of Evidence to rewrite your story

Ask yourself, *How will I know I'm safe?* Think about your specific evidence that will let you know you have the safety and security you need.

- Remember 3 times in your life when you were scared and you did it anyway
- Write down 3 areas of your life where you did create your own safety and security
- Notice how you have always been able to provide for yourself
- Do a net worth statement to understand if your financial worries are really as dire as they may seem. You might be surprised to find that you are perfectly safe and resourceful enough to always make sure you're safe
- Notice how many examples you have in your life now that provide you with comfort and safety

I'm Not (Good) Enough

Step 1: Identify the language pattern that resonates most deeply for you

Most Common Variations on the wording:

- I'm not good enough; I'm not enough
- I'm not smart enough, I'm not lucky enough, I'm not pretty/ handsome enough, (all other variations of this.)
- I'm not in the best shape right now; I'm not slim / fit enough
- I'm not sure I could do that
- I don't know if I have what it takes
- I feel like I'll never be enough to make you / them happy
- They're better off without me

Step 2: Identify your subconscious strategies that relate to this belief

- False bravado; overinflated sense of ego and self-importance
- Imposter syndrome – always feeling like you need a facade to project an image of yourself that's more attractive, more powerful; inability to just be yourself
- Never letting anyone get close enough to you that they find out who you really are
- Need for constant company or attention
- Overly flirtatious behavior, need for constant validation
- Lack of healthy boundaries
- Always needing to be the center of attention

Step 3: Find Examples of Evidence to rewrite your story

- Notice how many people are around you that love you for you
- Write down 3 or more great success stories or victories in your life that clearly indicate you are enough
- Notice 3 events where this belief stopped you from having what you truly desired. Now notice how different your choices would have been if you truly believed you are enough

Recall our example of Richard, the global CEO, who was extremely successful in business but not so successful in love. His deep need for validation was so big, it overruled his capacity to have normal friendships and a truly wholehearted and loving relationship. Unless he was able to recover from his past traumatic beliefs, he would have continued to have shallow, transactional relationships that stroked his ego versus provide him with the real love he craved. Richard is finally doing the work to recover from his past and has found a woman that loves him as he heals. His friendships now have healthier boundaries and he has found more balance in his life.

TOOL #3: Meditation—Retrain Your State Of Calm

Primary Intervention for Spiritual / Energetic & Emotional Bodies

Secondary Bodies affected: Mental & Physical Bodies

"The thing about meditation is you become more and more you."

—**David Lynch,** American Filmmaker, Chairman of the David Lynch Foundation, for Consciousness-Based Education and World Peace

A quick recap on meditation: Over the past few decades, the benefits of regular meditation have been well proven.[61] As we stated earlier, benefits include decreased stress, improved focus, boosted immunity, lower blood pressure, and reduced symptoms of anxiety and depression, just to name a few. While there are different types of meditation, they can all offer a similar set of proven benefits for mental and physical health. In terms of emotional well-being, meditation lessens worry and impulsivity, reduces fear and loneliness, enhances self-esteem and self-acceptance, improves resilience against pain and adversity, increases optimism, self-awareness and relaxation. Meditation helps develop positive social connections, improves your mood and increases emotional intelligence.

The trick with meditation is to find a way to practice that resonates with you. You can find a guided meditation like the one I created for you in the GetZENd app or you can sit in silence if that feels better for you. Many people I've spoken to over the years find it very difficult to just sit still and sit in silence. If you feel like you have trouble quieting your thoughts, don't resist them or make yourself wrong—just breathe through it. Allow your thoughts, observe them, then breathe and refocus on being still.

I actually don't use silent meditation in the morning. By that I mean, I prefer to focus on how I want to feel and then I focus on my goals and do a visualization meditation. I developed these same methods into guided meditations so you have an easy set of tools to accompany you on this journey. It takes the guesswork out of meditation. Just go to **www.getzend.com** and download the app for Apple or Android. Each meditation is specifically crafted to help you get the most desirable outcome, incorporating many of the tools from neuroscience and the study of success to help you do this if you're new to meditation.

The GetZENd app has a guided track called "Get Meditating," which will take you through specific cues of how to focus your breath, on the tension and release of tension in your body, and on various areas of your life. The app is designed to help you learn how to meditate and retrain your brain. It uses a blend of tools from neuroscience and hypnotherapy as well as sound wave technology to "tune in" to a desired relaxed brainwave. From there, you will be guided into a meditation where you can focus on different areas of your life, or you can choose to just listen to the brainwave music and enter a calmer state of mind.

For some people, meditation is more easily found when they connect with nature, like taking a walk on the beach or a walk in the woods. For others, they can sit peacefully in the sunshine or imagine themselves in their happy place, or a relaxed state. However you choose to do it is fine. If you can sit in silence and quiet the mind, then you're ahead of the game. I was not one of the lucky ones. I needed some training to just be comfortable with it, let alone find a way to do it that worked for me. This led me to develop the app so it was easier for you.

3 simple ways to begin your meditation practice:

1. ELEVATED EMOTION MEDITATION: Sit in a comfortable position. 6 deep breaths with a slow exhale will trigger your body to enter a calmer state. With every exhale, allow the tension in your body to just relax and release. There's nowhere else you need to be now. Next, just focus on 3 feelings and really allow your self to either

remember moments when you felt that emotion or imagine new moments you'd like to create. The ones that work for me are peaceful, happy, and calm. As you think of each one, imagine a series of different moments. As you do this you are stringing together powerful positive emotions and thoughts and actions (what you're doing) in those moments. Remember to embody the feelings until they are flowing through you. If you can spend 10-20 minutes just on what you want to feel, that's already working to retrain and rewire the brain for greater joy, less stress, and more peace.

2. RELAXATION MEDITATION: Lay down in a comfortable position. 6 deep breaths with a slow exhale will trigger your body to enter a calmer state. With every exhale, allow the tension in your body to just relax and release. There's nowhere else you need to be now. Next, just do a scan of your body and notice any areas of tension. With each inhale, breathe in gentle peaceful energy, with every exhale, release tension in that area.
    - Relax your forehead, your brow, your cheeks and your jaw... notice how tightly you held that and just allow it to release
    - Next, relax your neck, your shoulders, your arms and allow your shoulders to drop
    - Relax the muscles in your upper back, your lower back, your abdomen
    - Allow all the muscles in your thighs, your knees, your calves and feet to relax too
    - Just be in this restful place, picturing the most tranquil scene you can imagine
    - If you wish, allow yourself to drift off to a deep, sound sleep

3. GUIDED MEDITATION: This is the easiest way to meditate for those who are new or have tried it but have not found their own rhythm with it. I've specially developed an app that incorporates all of the science discussed in this book, to help you realign your four bodies and easily cultivate a daily practice. Simply go to **www.getzend.**

com and Download the **GetZENd app** for Apple or Android. In the app, you will find a whole range of guided meditations specifically designed to get you into a desired state of mind. Here you will find tracks to help you ***Get Focused***, ***Get Goals***, ***Get Meditating***, and ***Get Into the Performance Zone***. You will also find tracks for ***Stress Relief*** and ***Deep Healing***, to help you through a mind-body healing visualization exercise, and you will find how to ***Get Unplugged*** and ***Get Deep Sleep***. Each track is written with specific language patterns and uses a technology called binaural beats, to tune your brain waves into the right frequency. From there, all you have to do is breathe and relax.

The 6 Weeks to Happy Assessment

1. SLEEP QUALITY: 1☐ 2☐ 3☐
   Rate the quality of your sleep from 1 to 3, where 1 is Fair (less than 4 hours per night), 2 is Good (4 to 6 hours per night) and 3 is Great (7 or more hours per night)

2. TENSION IN THE BODY
   1☐ 2☐ 3☐

   Rate your level of tension in the body from 1 to 3, where 1 is Fair (breathing is labored, muscles are tight and tense in the neck and shoulders), 2 is Good (breathing is good, some tension in the neck and shoulders) and 3 is Great (breathing is relaxed and the body is no longer holding onto too much stress related tension)

3. ABILITY TO MANAGE ENERGY:
   1☐ 2☐ 3☐
   Rate your ability to manage and regulate your energy levels throughout the week, where 1 is Fair (very tired, not enough time and energy to do everything you need), 2 is Good (a bit tired, but getting better at prioritizing and managing your energy balance) and 3 is Great (sometimes tired, and overall doing well at re-prioritizing and making time to recharge)

4. ABILITY TO REGULATE MOOD & EMOTIONS:
   1☐ 2☐ 3☐
   Rate your ability to regulate your mood and emotions from 1 to 3, where 1 is Fair (irritable or easily agitated, short-tempered), 2 is Good (sometimes irritable or agitated), 3 is Great (able to choose your reactions more and stay calm)

5. STRESS LEVEL: 1☐ 2☐ 3☐
   Rate your stress level from 1 to 3, where 1 is Fair (moderate levels of worry, anxiety throughout the day), 2 is Good (low levels of worry and anxiety) and 3 is Great (knowing all is well and you're coping well)

6. FEELINGS OF HAPPINESS: 1☐ 2☐ 3☐
   Rate your feelings of happiness from 1 to 3, where 1 is Fair (infrequent feelings of hope, love, gratitude, joy, peace mixed with anxiety and worry), 2 is Good (frequent feelings of hope, love, gratitude, joy, peace) and 3 is Great (spending most of the day with feelings of happiness and a sense of grace and ease)

Week 2:
E = ELIMINATE THE NOISE

TOOL #1:
Review Your Budget

Primary Intervention for Mental & Emotional Bodies

Secondary Body affected: Physical Body

Energy In must equal Energy Out in a given week to keep us feeling good, to feel like we are moving through life with ease. Think of it like a bank account for energy. You only have a finite amount to spend each week before you're tapped out. Your sense of willpower can give you an indication for how you're doing and make sure you don't make too many withdrawals.

You must find ways of restoring your energy in a given week by making deposits into your energy account before you start spending energy the next week or you'll be running on empty.

Let's review your Energy Budget:

1. Take note of the necessary actions that need your attention each week – work, family, other responsibilities.
2. Now, look at areas of your life where you are spending time and

energy that are of less importance and define 3 or more activities where you could pull back a bit to regain that equilibrium. For example, can you reduce the number of social events or time spent with people or activities that drain you?

3. Take note of the things that restore and recharge you. Sleep is the most obvious way we recharge. Don't forget about the activities that may take energy but also replenish, like exercise and other cathartic activities which allow you to release tension.

TOOL #2:
Eliminate The Noise in Your Life

Primary Intervention for Mental & Emotional Bodies

Secondary Body affected: Physical Body

Once you assess your energy account you will notice if there are extraneous activities draining you of resources. It's time to stop engaging in activities and spending time with people that don't bring value to your life and drain you of your energy.

Start by being conscious of how you're feeling in each moment—Where are you? What are you doing? Who are you with? Then begin asking the following questions:

- Do I feel at peace, joyful, calm?
- Does each person here make me feel at ease or is it challenging to be around them?
- Am I truly enjoying what I'm doing with my time?
- What is right about this situation? What is wrong about this situation?
- What about this situation does not resonate for me or make me feel like I'm living my best life?

Try using the same metric for weeding people and situations out of your life that are depleting your energy bank account. Remember, "Just as someone's bad mood can rub off on you, positivity, too, may spread." If you're taking the time to find your way to happiness, then you have a right to choose how and with whom you want to spend your time.

Many people feel obligated to family members or old friends that require a lot of us. If there's an activity, social scene or a person that makes you feel drained, just notice it for now. Understand you get to choose how much time and energy you give away.

1. Take note of up to three situations where your energy tends toward the negative versus the positive. For example, spending too much time online or watching the news can be disturbing. An easy fix is to timebox the amount of time to spend reviewing the world's current events. You can set specific times where you get to check email and social media. Rather than constantly checking your phone, just do it at the top of the hour, handle the urgent business, then unplug. Another fix includes noticing how a colleague or friend might take more energy than you have to give that week and find ways to reschedule for when you have it to give.
2. Start to draw healthy boundaries to remove yourself or to minimize the time spent in situations that could otherwise be draining or negative.
3. Take note of 3 things you could do to bring more joy, more peace, more relaxation, and more fun into your week.
4. Take note of 3 things you can do to recharge and replenish your energy stores throughout the week.

Just like when you make time to do a spring cleaning of your house or closet, it's time to really examine your life and ask yourself what brings you joy and what is just taking up space? Draw healthy boundaries so you have enough time to look after yourself and those that matter most. Know that you absolutely have the right to choose the people and activities in your life. Choosing to spend time in situations that leave you feeling uplifted will strengthen your ability to stay in a state of calm and will give you greater energy.

TOOL #3:
Balance Your Budget, Balance Your Life

Primary Intervention for Mental, Emotional & Physical Bodies

What brings you joy and what's just taking up space? Ask yourself some of these questions:

- How can you revise your schedule so you aren't at zero in your energy account at the end of the week?
- What small changes can you make so you aren't running on empty?
- What changes can you make so that you are depositing energy back into your balance each week?
- What are some of the activities that restore and deplete your energy?

A quick recap of the most common sources of energy:

- Getting enough sleep (6-8 hours minimum)
- A balanced diet, staying well hydrated
- Regular exercise
- Support from family and friends
- Spending time alone—with no demands for your time and energy

As you learn to make room for more restorative activities, put them into practice more regularly. You will find you're naturally calmer, less stressed and able to experience more joy in each day because you are better able to be truly present. You're not stretched too thin anymore.

Let's take a look at some of the key indicators for balance in the four bodies:

- You wake up feeling more rested
- You have more even energy throughout the day
- You are more in control of your emotional state

- Your stress level seems manageable
- Your sleep quality is improving
- You have better willpower as needed
- You have greater focus and clarity

As you balance your energy budget, try to make time for more replenishing activities.

See if you can reprioritize your week's activities, so you are able to do what is necessary while spending time with fun, playful activities that bring you greater joy and laughter. Be sure to include more time to rest and activities that restore your energy.

The 6 Weeks to Happy Assessment

1. SLEEP QUALITY: 1☐ 2☐ 3☐
   Rate the quality of your sleep from 1 to 3, where 1 is Fair (less than 4 hours per night), 2 is Good (4 to 6 hours per night) and 3 is Great (7 or more hours per night)

2. TENSION IN THE BODY
   1☐ 2☐ 3☐
   Rate your level of tension in the body from 1 to 3, where 1 is Fair (breathing is labored, muscles are tight and tense in the neck and shoulders), 2 is Good (breathing is good, some tension in the neck and shoulders) and 3 is Great (breathing is relaxed and the body is no longer holding onto too much stress related tension)

3. ABILITY TO MANAGE ENERGY:
   1☐ 2☐ 3☐
   Rate your ability to manage and regulate your energy levels throughout the week, where 1 is Fair (very tired, not enough time and energy to do everything you need), 2 is Good (a bit tired, but getting better at prioritizing and managing your energy balance) and 3 is Great (sometimes tired, and overall doing well at re-prioritizing and making time to recharge)

4. ABILITY TO REGULATE MOOD & EMOTIONS:
   1☐ 2☐ 3☐
   Rate your ability to regulate your mood and emotions from 1 to 3, where 1 is Fair (irritable or easily agitated, short-tempered), 2 is Good (sometimes irritable or agitated), 3 is Great (able to choose your reactions more and stay calm)

5. STRESS LEVEL: 1☐ 2☐ 3☐
   Rate your stress level from 1 to 3, where 1 is Fair (moderate levels of worry, anxiety throughout the day), 2 is Good (low levels of worry and anxiety) and 3 is Great (knowing all is well and you're coping well)

6. FEELINGS OF HAPPINESS: 1☐ 2☐ 3☐
   Rate your feelings of happiness from 1 to 3, where 1 is Fair (infrequent feelings of hope, love, gratitude, joy, peace mixed with anxiety and worry), 2 is Good (frequent feelings of hope, love, gratitude, joy, peace) and 3 is Great (spending most of the day with feelings of happiness and a sense of grace and ease)

Week 3:

W = WHAT DO YOU NEED?

TOOL #1:

Pay Attention To What Makes You Feel Most Alive

Primary Intervention for Mental & Emotional Bodies

Secondary Bodies Affected: Physical and Spiritual / Energetic bodies.

Think of the moments in life when you felt the most excited, energized and alive. Those were moments during or immediately after you had your needs met! It could have happened during a great workout, or strolling outdoors as you breathed in the fresh air and took in the sights and sounds of nature. It could've been during a beautiful quiet night to yourself or when you went out with friends. Take a minute now to think of a few of these moments in your life.

- Identify 3-5 times in your life when you felt happiest.
  - Write down every detail you can remember. Where were you? Who were you with? What were you doing? Start to notice if there was something specific in each moment that really made you feel great. Was it the scenery? The home? The type of connection? Your state of health?
- Identify up to 3 times in your life when you felt really powerful like you were certain you could do anything!

- Notice all the little details in these moments too. What was your state of mind? What was your physical health like at that time? What is it about what you were doing then that made you feel so certain?

- Identify at least 5 times in your life when you knew you were really content, fulfilled, peaceful.
    - Write down what you were doing in those moments and the details you can recall. Were you feeling loved? Were you engaged in something you feel passionate about, or were you simply doing something for which you have a natural talent, like when you're in the state of flow?

TOOL #2:
Define Your Core Needs

Primary Intervention for All Four Bodies - Spiritual/ Energetic, Mental, Emotional & Physical bodies

Take a look at your notes from the Needs Analysis and compile them into one list so you can see your needs clearly in the following categories:

1. **Physical**—How much food, water, exercise, sleep, fresh air do you need to feel great?
2. **Social**—Are you a social butterfly? How often do you like to see friends and family? Are you comfortable socializing alone or with a partner or friend?
3. **Mental & Intellectual** —What sort of mental, intellectual and creative stimulation do you need in order to feel excited and inspired—books, podcasts, documentaries, films, galleries or exhibits, engaging in stimulating conversation? New information and learning new skills stimulate the mind. What might satisfy your passions? Painting, dance and language classes? History classes or acquiring a new skill?
4. **Emotional (Affection, Love, Sex)**—Are you having your needs met in your primary relationship with yourself? In your

secondary relationship with your partner? Are you getting the support and type of support you need?

5. **Financial**—In order to feel like you have no worries and anxiety about the future, get really specific on what you need to have financial security.
6. **Soulful & Spiritual**—What are your spiritual needs? What makes you feel calm, serene, at peace, grounded? What makes you feel like you have meaning in your life? Are you living in alignment with who you truly are?

TOOL #3:

How Can You Have More Of Your Needs Met More Often?

Primary Intervention for All Four Bodies - Spiritual/ Energetic, Mental, Emotional & Physical bodies

- Review your list of needs and notice how NOT having them met has made you feel over time? Write it down so you have this as a reference.
- Schedule at least five things over the next four weeks so that you are having more of your needs met by the time you finish this book.
- Notice how much more joyful, relaxed, peaceful and excited you can be about your life.

Once you make a few simple changes and commit to having more of your needs fulfilled then you can live life with more ease. You will hear yourself exhale and feel more relaxed. Almost immediately, you will experience instant relief knowing that you've decided to choose your life and live the life that makes you happier. Once you've identified your needs and scheduled them, life becomes immensely more satisfying and can be lived with greater ease.

The 6 Weeks to Happy Assessment

1. SLEEP QUALITY: 1☐ 2☐ 3☐
   Rate the quality of your sleep from 1 to 3, where 1 is Fair (less than 4 hours per night), 2 is Good (4 to 6 hours per night) and 3 is Great (7 or more hours per night)

2. TENSION IN THE BODY
   1☐ 2☐ 3☐

   Rate your level of tension in the body from 1 to 3, where 1 is Fair (breathing is labored, muscles are tight and tense in the neck and shoulders), 2 is Good (breathing is good, some tension in the neck and shoulders) and 3 is Great (breathing is relaxed and the body is no longer holding onto too much stress related tension)

3. ABILITY TO MANAGE ENERGY:
   1☐ 2☐ 3☐
   Rate your ability to manage and regulate your energy levels throughout the week, where 1 is Fair (very tired, not enough time and energy to do everything you need), 2 is Good (a bit tired, but getting better at prioritizing and managing your energy balance) and 3 is Great (sometimes tired, and overall doing well at re-prioritizing and making time to recharge)

4. ABILITY TO REGULATE MOOD & EMOTIONS:
   1☐ 2☐ 3☐
   Rate your ability to regulate your mood and emotions from 1 to 3, where 1 is Fair (irritable or easily agitated, short-tempered), 2 is Good (sometimes irritable or agitated), 3 is Great (able to choose your reactions more and stay calm)

5. STRESS LEVEL: 1☐ 2☐ 3☐
   Rate your stress level from 1 to 3, where 1 is Fair (moderate levels of worry, anxiety throughout the day), 2 is Good (low levels of worry and anxiety) and 3 is Great (knowing all is well and you're coping well)

6. FEELINGS OF HAPPINESS: 1☐ 2☐ 3☐
   Rate your feelings of happiness from 1 to 3, where 1 is Fair (infrequent feelings of hope, love, gratitude, joy, peace mixed with anxiety and worry), 2 is Good (frequent feelings of hope, love, gratitude, joy, peace) and 3 is Great (spending most of the day with feelings of happiness and a sense of grace and ease)

Week 4:

I = IMAGINE & VISUALIZE A NEW FUTURE

This week is about developing a deeper sense of self-awareness so you have more clarity about what is working well and discarding what is not. Once you start to develop a clearer image of what you want to create in your life and how you want to feel, then you can begin taking action and using visualization to help the brain rehearse, rewire the brain to your new life, and hardwire a new mindset so that your reality aligns too.

TOOL #1:
Define Your Top Five Values

Primary Intervention for Mental & Emotional Bodies

We talked earlier about how values are what's important to you. They are the guiding principles for how you interact with people and situations when you're being your most authentic self. Just like needs, when we are not living in alignment with what we value most, how could we possibly be living our best life? Now you get to go deeper.

Have a look at the list below and just try each value on to see if it resonates with you. Ask yourself—*How important are each of these values to me? How would I feel if I didn't have this in my life?* As you go through the list, you'll start to discover areas of your personality that are more important than others and distinguish the values you cannot live without. While this is a well-rounded list, there may be a few more that you identify with that are not on this list. In this case, feel free to define your own and follow along with the exercise.

- ☐ Achievement
- ☐ Adventure
- ☐ Autonomy
- ☐ Compassion
- ☐ Courage
- ☐ Creativity
- ☐ Determination
- ☐ Excitement
- ☐ Friendship
- ☐ Freedom
- ☐ Health
- ☐ Honesty
- ☐ Independence
- ☐ Integrity
- ☐ Intelligence
- ☐ Justice
- ☐ Kindness
- ☐ Learning
- ☐ Love
- ☐ Peace
- ☐ Perfection
- ☐ Routine
- ☐ Security
- ☐ Simplicity
- ☐ Sincerity
- ☐ Spontaneity
- ☐ Success
- ☐ Understanding
- ☐ Wealth

Define your top five values, the permeating themes that you wish to include in every aspect of your life—from your relationships to your work, and how you wish to spend your time in between.

- Identify your Top 5 Values - what's most important to you.
- As you look at your Top 5 Values, notice how not having those values met in your life has made you feel in specific situations. Write it down so you can recall this at a later date and stay aligned to what really matters most to you.
- Next, write down at least one way you can have your values included in each area of your life.
- Keep extending this work as often as you can by revisiting and realigning with your values more and more.

TOOL #2:
Practice Focusing On The Outcome You Want

Primary Intervention for Mental & Emotional Bodies

Secondary Bodies affected: Spiritual/Energetic & Physical Bodies

Instead of worrying about all the things that could go wrong in your plan or your goals, practice focusing on the outcome you want and how you will feel when you get there. If that feels too big, then you can break the goal up into micro-goals—smaller milestones that you can accomplish on your way. You can also focus on any known obstacles and imagine yourself overcoming those.

Remember, there are two powerful types of visualization—Process Visualization and Outcome Visualization. Process Visualization is where you allow yourself to imagine the steps along the way to achieving your outcome. Outcome Visualization is seeing yourself in that moment when you will have already achieved it. Use both of these tools as you imagine each of your new goals, aligned with your values, and conquering the challenges until you reach the end state you desire.

- As you think of your top 5 values, allow yourself to sit and daydream a bit—this is another way to practice visualization. Just imagine, for example, how it would *feel* to be *free.* Free of all your worries, absolutely certain you have all you'll ever need, knowing your family is looked after, your bills are paid, you're planning next year's vacations, free to choose work that you love, free to be yourself, love how you like.
- As often as you can throughout the day, only focus on the positive outcome you wish to see in your life. Focus entirely on the intention and all those wonderful feelings that go with it. The more you do this, the more you rewire your brain and your reality to how you want to feel.

TOOL #3:
Use Visualization To Imagine This New Life

Primary Intervention for All Four Bodies to be in Harmony

Spiritual/Energetic, Mental, Emotional & Physical Bodies

Using Visualization, begin to create new neurology and string together several moments *in each category of needs* so that you have the IDEAL scenario built-in. Imagine specific moments as though you already have what you desire. What are you DOING? Are you turning the key to your new home? Are you having a joyful moment with your family? Are you standing on a sandy beach? Get a really clear V-A-K representation—Visual, Auditory, Kinesthetic. What do you SEE? What do you HEAR? What do you FEEL in that moment where you already have a new reality for love, health, prosperity, connection, happiness?

- Look at the Areas of your life in Week 3's exercise. Start to imagine specific moments in each area of your life, making sure your needs are met and that you're aligned with your values.
  - As you imagine each moment, make sure to get a crystal clear image of what you hope to achieve. As you do so, see very clearly what you are doing in the moments when you already have achieved it. What are you doing? What do you see, hear and feel in each moment?
  - Now string together 3 or more moments for each outcome you'd like to achieve. The more thoughts and feelings you can string together, the deeper you will connect new neurology and begin to create a new future for yourself.
- Use Visualization at the start of the day. You can do it in addition to your morning meditation or if you're using the GetZENd app, then you already have them included in your meditations.
- A simple visualization to do on your own:
  - Start with how you want to feel (you can use your values here too).
  - Next, focus on your health and wellbeing.
  - Go outward to visualize your ideal partner or relationship. It doesn't matter if you are single or in a relationship, you can still practice how you want it to feel. Imagine little moments that would have you feel loved and adored, safe, protected, cherished in every way. Imagine how you want your relationship to look. What will you be doing? How do you want to make each other feel?
  - Next, you can picture your family and social circle. What do you want to be doing? How do you want to feel?
  - Then look at your work, imagine doing it with passion, excitement, and meaning.
  - Picture your whole life in little moments just as you would want it.

The 6 Weeks to Happy Assessment

1. SLEEP QUALITY: 1☐ 2☐ 3☐
Rate the quality of your sleep from 1 to 3, where 1 is Fair (less than 4 hours per night), 2 is Good (4 to 6 hours per night) and 3 is Great (7 or more hours per night)

2. TENSION IN THE BODY
1☐ 2☐ 3☐
Rate your level of tension in the body from 1 to 3, where 1 is Fair (breathing is labored, muscles are tight and tense in the neck and shoulders), 2 is Good (breathing is good, some tension in the neck and shoulders) and 3 is Great (breathing is relaxed and the body is no longer holding onto too much stress related tension)

3. ABILITY TO MANAGE ENERGY:
1☐ 2☐ 3☐
Rate your ability to manage and regulate your energy levels throughout the week, where 1 is Fair (very tired, not enough time and energy to do everything you need), 2 is Good (a bit tired, but getting better at prioritizing and managing your energy balance) and 3 is Great (sometimes tired, and overall doing well at re-prioritizing and making time to recharge)

4. ABILITY TO REGULATE MOOD & EMOTIONS:
1☐ 2☐ 3☐
Rate your ability to regulate your mood and emotions from 1 to 3, where 1 is Fair (irritable or easily agitated, short-tempered), 2 is Good (sometimes irritable or agitated), 3 is Great (able to choose your reactions more and stay calm)

5. STRESS LEVEL: 1☐ 2☐ 3☐
Rate your stress level from 1 to 3, where 1 is Fair (moderate levels of worry, anxiety throughout the day), 2 is Good (low levels of worry and anxiety) and 3 is Great (knowing all is well and you're coping well)

6. FEELINGS OF HAPPINESS: 1☐ 2☐ 3☐
Rate your feelings of happiness from 1 to 3, where 1 is Fair (infrequent feelings of hope, love, gratitude, joy, peace mixed with anxiety and worry), 2 is Good (frequent feelings of hope, love, gratitude, joy, peace) and 3 is Great (spending most of the day with feelings of happiness and a sense of grace and ease)

Week 5:
R = REPEAT & REWIRE

Taking some time at the start of each day to focus on how you want to feel begins the day on the right foot. Continuing to do this throughout the day keeps you in the right state of mind—*consciously choosing what to think, what to feel and choosing the actions that will rewire for long-lasting and enduring change.* If we want to build new habits, new thought patterns, and new emotions that align with a happier and more exciting and peaceful life, let's start the cycle at the top of each day and stay in the zone to repeat and rewire.

TOOL #1: Set Your Intentions for the Day

Primary Intervention for Mental & Emotional Bodies

Secondary Body affected: Spiritual/Energetic Body

"Our Intention Creates our Reality."

—**Dr. Wayne Dyer,** International Author & Speaker in the fields of Self Development & Spiritual Growth

- Start by thinking about what you need to accomplish today.
- Focus on how you want to feel in each moment. For example, I love to start the day feeling peaceful, filled with gratitude and excited

about what I get to do. Throughout the day, I want tons of energy and focus, so I can be really productive. In the evening I want enough energy to be able to enjoy some recreation and laughter. At the end of the day, I want to lay in bed, totally relaxed, knowing I accomplished everything I wanted to and fall asleep feeling happy and grateful.

- Imagine all the resources you need to show up just as you need.
- Imagine yourself walking through the day with ease. Whatever meetings you have, picture them all going extremely well. Start your day by focusing on how you want to *feel*, then how you imagine your day going so that it's just what you need. Imagine yourself feeling *happy, peaceful, calm, then imagine everything you need in your day coming together easily and effortlessly.*
- Now that you're beginning your day with meditation, you can do this at the same time by focusing on what you'd like to create.
- Sit with your coffee or just sit for five minutes at the start of the day and focus on very specific images of what you'd like to create in your life. *Always imagine.*
  - *What will you see, hear and feel once you've accomplished your goal successfully?* Imagine several moments for each goal being accomplished.
  - Imagine yourself in perfect health at any age.
  - Imagine specific moments in your relationships and how you want to feel.
  - Imagine your social and community life.
  - Imagine your work and career goals as you achieve them.
  - Imagine a life filled with meaning.
  - Imagine yourself feeling fulfilled.
- If you're using the GetZENd app, then you have three tools combined into one. The meditations are designed to help you meditate, practice visualization, and set your intentions for the day. Just as the brain is designed for efficiency, so am I—like wanting things to be quick, easy and simple. Use the GetZENd app to start your day off right by hitting three tools in one.

Whatever these moments look like for you, imagine yourself moving through the day and through each milestone with grace and ease, feeling completely loved, peaceful, and excited. As you visualize, include moments where your values are laced in. If you want freedom, then include moments where you feel free of worry and constraints or however that looks for you. Imagine yourself in each moment having endless options and the ability to choose whatever you desire.

You'll also find more energy in your day because you're not starting the day off on autopilot. You are starting your day by consciously choosing how you want to feel, think and behave. To make it even easier for you, I've carefully built this type of visualization into the guided meditations in the GetZend app. You get to meditate, visualize and set your intentions for the day, all at the same time, by doing this in the morning. Start your day off right and everything will just feel easier.

TOOL #2: The R.E.W.I.R.E. Triad™

Primary Intervention for Mental & Emotional Bodies

Secondary Bodies affected: Spiritual/Energetic & Physical Bodies

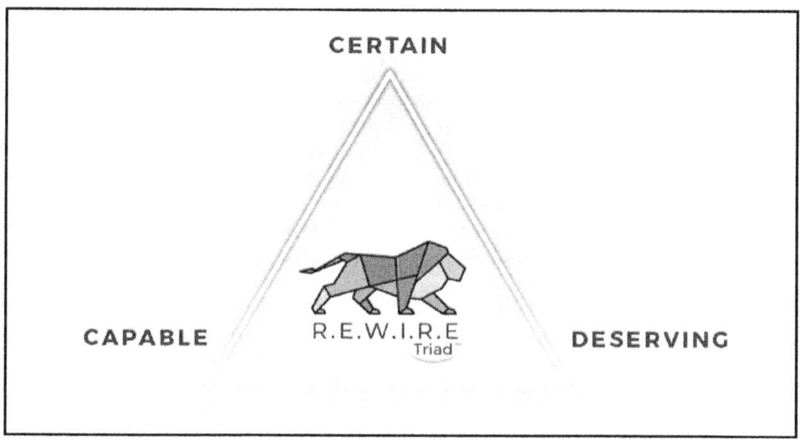

In order to rewire away from our survival based beliefs—the 5 Main Limiting Core Beliefs—we need to install a new operating language. Years of programming to those subconscious beliefs can be rewritten so that we can return to a mindset of certainty, love and abundance. This is a great starting point to begin healing old patterns of thinking and feeling and take our power back.

Some of that old trauma requires deeper healing and may need you to do more inner work or get individual coaching. See the Resource Center at the end of this book for a reference for deeper healing and also check out www.getzend.com for more on coaching resources and to download the GetZEND app.

Rebalancing the effects of the 5 Main Limiting Core Beliefs is the first step to getting control over our old survival patterns and over those old thought and feeling loops that no longer serve you. If we can get ahead of the thoughts and feelings that would normally derail you and begin putting in place new thoughts and feelings, then you can begin rewiring a new neurology that leaves you feeling more empowered. We are essentially laying the foundation for a new, healing, limitless version of you.

The R.E.W.I.R.E. Triad™ is how we overcome our limiting core beliefs. Again, here are the most common 5 Main Limiting Core Beliefs:

- I'm Not Loved (or I'm Unworthy of Being Loved)
- I'm Undeserving of Wealth or Success or a life I love
- I'm Alone (or Unsupported)
- I'm Not Safe (or not Protected)
- I'm Not (Good) Enough

The R.E.W.I.R.E. Triad™ consists of three groups of thoughts and feelings that begin to restore you back to wholeness. The R.E.W.I.R.E. Triad™ also includes a series of affirmations that shift your inner knowing back to feeling *certain, capable,* and *deserving.*

- Recite each statement either quietly to yourself or aloud.
- As you go through each affirmation, *feel* into it and embody the vibration that goes with it.
- Repeat each one a few times, until you feel it wash over you and begin to rewrite your subconscious beliefs. As you do so, you are rewriting that neurology while eliminating the old patterns that no longer serve you. As you practice, you will see, hear or feel a change as it shifts back to wholeness. You will feel the integration happening within you as you start to embody love, certainty and abundance again.

For example, when you say *I am certain that I am loved and fully supported in every way,* allow that feeling of love and support to vibrate through you. Repeat it over and over until you embody it with complete confidence. When you say, *I am capable of accomplishing my goals with ease and grace,* allow that feeling of ease to wash over you. When you say *I am deserving of the highest love and of all the abundance the universe has for me,* allow that to light you up totally. Allow yourself to see, hear and feel everything until the old ways of being no longer have a tight hold on you. Allow this new language pattern to sink into your subconscious, creating your new reality.

Remember that the power of language—your language especially—is a suggestion to your subconscious mind. The more careful and intentional you are with your words, the more you are rewiring yourself for more love, greater connection, better health, more abundance, more meaning, and greater fulfillment. As you invite more compassionate and abundant words into your vocabulary, you will begin to create a new reality for yourself.

A quick recap: Feeling more *certain, capable, and deserving* is the foundation of how we can create change in our life. If we have a deep understanding that we are *certain, capable* and *deserving* of love in the highest form, of being in the optimal state of health, of being fully connected to God or source energy, of always being completely supported, then we are reprogramming away from fear and self-doubt. We are able to program away from survival mode and step into our own power and live life with happiness and purpose.

The R.E.W.I.R.E. Triad™ is about getting out of the old states of our being which yield the same results over time, leaving us with all the symptoms of not showing up in our lives—exhaustion, depression and depletion. Instead, we choose to embrace a new state of being where we are enough, where we are loved, supported, safe, and deserving of all the happiness and prosperity we can handle. Our new thoughts, feelings and behaviors build on each other and soon we are enjoying the experiences that fill us up and create more calm, peace and happiness in our lives. This new state of being brings new results.

R.E.W.I.R.E. Triad™ Affirmations

Recite and Embody Each One.

- I am enough. I am whole. I have everything I need to create the life of my dreams and to have a life of meaning. I am perfect and beautiful and talented just as I am. I am in perfect health and timeless at any age. I welcome love, peace, joy, laughter, adventure and abundance into my life in the most amazing ways.
- I am loved. I am worthy of giving and receiving love wholeheartedly, with trust, adoration, passion, joy, partnership & connection in every way. I invite all the relationships I need into my life. I know that I am surrounded by love in all moments.
- I know I am always connected to source and surrounded by love & protection. I welcome love & guidance into my life. I am certain. I trust myself. I put my trust in God and the Universe that everything is always happening for my highest good. I am fully supported in all moments.

- I am safe. I am strong. I am secure & capable in every way. I am certain that I am always supported, guided & protected. I trust myself, my intuition and the universe to help me make choices for the highest good. I know I will always be provided for and looked after in the most miraculous ways.
- I am deserving of love, connection and abundance. I am deserving of wealth, love & prosperity in every way. I am open to receive all my blessings & all the miracles meant for me. I trust that I am always looked after in the most abundant ways.

TOOL #3: Commit To A Daily Practice

Primary Intervention for All Four Bodies to be in Harmony

Spiritual / Energetic, Mental, Emotional & Physical Bodies

To repeat and rewire, we need to operate from a state of calm. The easiest way to do this is to begin each day in a state of calm—in that deep knowing that you are safe, you are supported, you are loved and always looked after in the most abundant ways. As you begin your day with meditation, visualization and setting your intentions, you already have a morning routine. If you're using the GetZENd app, then you're doing all three at once.

- Spend at least 10-20 minutes at the start of the day to practice conscious thought and feeling.
- Work your way up to 20 minutes or more each day. The more you practice this new conscious way of being, the quicker and more powerful it will be. Find a few activities that allow you to begin your day in this new mindset and can keep you in this new state of being all day.
- Practice Returning to Calm with deep breathing—at least 6 deep breaths to trigger your parasympathetic nervous system to return to calm.

Remember, when you find yourself in a state of stress, you can actively return to a state of calm by practicing deep breathing. When it comes to effective maneuvers, any type of deep, slow diaphragm breathing—during which you visualize filling up the lower part of your lungs just above your belly button like a balloon, and then exhaling slowly—is going to stimulate your vagus nerve. This activates your parasympathetic nervous system which controls your natural, calmer state.

Life happens, and events will trigger stress. This is a breathing technique you can use to quickly bring you back to balance. You can do this at any time to help you return to your natural state of rest-and-digest. The more you breathe deeply, the more quickly you can go from feeling stressed to feeling relaxed. As you master this technique, you rewire your neurology to not only return to this calm state more quickly, but you will also find you spend more time there, leaving you in a better state of overall health, happiness, and in greater tune with your intuition so you can make decisions and choices that are inline with your core values.

The 6 Weeks to Happy Assessment

1. SLEEP QUALITY: 1☐ 2☐ 3☐
   Rate the quality of your sleep from 1 to 3, where 1 is Fair (less than 4 hours per night), 2 is Good (4 to 6 hours per night) and 3 is Great (7 or more hours per night)

2. TENSION IN THE BODY
   1☐ 2☐ 3☐

   Rate your level of tension in the body from 1 to 3, where 1 is Fair (breathing is labored, muscles are tight and tense in the neck and shoulders), 2 is Good (breathing is good, some tension in the neck and shoulders) and 3 is Great (breathing is relaxed and the body is no longer holding onto too much stress related tension)

3. ABILITY TO MANAGE ENERGY:
   1☐ 2☐ 3☐
   Rate your ability to manage and regulate your energy levels throughout the week, where 1 is Fair (very tired, not enough time and energy to do everything you need), 2 is Good (a bit tired, but getting better at prioritizing and managing your energy balance) and 3 is Great (sometimes tired, and overall doing well at re-prioritizing and making time to recharge)

4. ABILITY TO REGULATE MOOD & EMOTIONS:
   1☐ 2☐ 3☐
   Rate your ability to regulate your mood and emotions from 1 to 3, where 1 is Fair (irritable or easily agitated, short-tempered), 2 is Good (sometimes irritable or agitated), 3 is Great (able to choose your reactions more and stay calm)

5. STRESS LEVEL: 1☐ 2☐ 3☐
   Rate your stress level from 1 to 3, where 1 is Fair (moderate levels of worry, anxiety throughout the day), 2 is Good (low levels of worry and anxiety) and 3 is Great (knowing all is well and you're coping well)

6. FEELINGS OF HAPPINESS: 1☐ 2☐ 3☐
   Rate your feelings of happiness from 1 to 3, where 1 is Fair (infrequent feelings of hope, love, gratitude, joy, peace mixed with anxiety and worry), 2 is Good (frequent feelings of hope, love, gratitude, joy, peace) and 3 is Great (spending most of the day with feelings of happiness and a sense of grace and ease)

Week 6:
E = ELEVATE & EXPAND

As you have learned, we are wired to pay more attention to the negative than we are to the positive. We evolved to have a heightened sense of attention to the negative in the event of danger. Even when there is no danger present, we still do this in life. The more we focus on the negative, the more we trigger our state of stress. To counteract this negativity bias, we need to actively and consciously light up our state of calm and remain positive. The following set of tools will help you do just that.

TOOL #1:
Cultivate Self-Love As The Foundation For Compassion

Primary Intervention for Spiritual / Energetic, Mental & Emotional Bodies

If other people matter and our relationships matter, then we also need to matter. We've talked about the necessity for healing past trauma and being able to arrive at a point where you can feel a sense of belonging here in this life, certainty that you are supported and loved, and deserving of respect and abundance in every way. The next step is to learn to be kinder to ourselves and turn that compassion inwards.

- **Extend and Expand the Positive Moments**

Take more time to focus on the positive things that happen *and all the wonderful emotions* that come with those moments.

> Celebrate those moments and the feelings that go with them! The more time you spend in these powerful positive emotional states, the more you rewire your brain for greater joy, fulfillment, and success.

> Relish your victories and all those delicious feelings that come with doing something well! When someone pays you a compliment or shines a light on you, don't just redirect and shift focus away! Allow yourself to let it in!

> Then, take as much time as you can throughout your day to focus on those emotions. From now on, when positive events happen, take a few *extra* moments to really feel the positive feelings that come with those events. This will also bring you back to a place of self love and appreciation.

- **Increase Your Daily Intake of Positive Emotions**

Instead of spending time ruminating, worrying and focusing on what goes wrong in our lives, we need to strengthen and build our ability to let in the good feelings.

> Beginning the day in a peaceful state of mind is a great start.

> Next, allow yourself to feel a sense of awe by savoring good moments when they happen.

> Allow yourself to revel in the wonder of YOU as well. Really look back at your journey. If you are reading this book, then I know you have come through so many challenges. Take a moment here to celebrate you—your bravery, your courage, your *willingness to overcome*. Celebrate your strength, all you've learned, your power, your beauty, your talents and how well you've handled it all.

- **Practice Gratitude as often as you can**

You can add this to your repertoire of positive emotions in the morning, and do this repeatedly, any time you are taking a break in the day. If you can finish the day feeling grateful, then it flows with you throughout the entire day and keeps you in an abundance mindset.

> When things go wrong, be grateful for what the experience taught you, then let go and reset. Keep the learning and discard the rest. This is a valuable lesson when things go wrong with people and events in your life. Being grateful for the learning experience—even when it can sometimes happen in a painful way—and learning how to leave the drama behind is a powerful skill to learn.

- **Mindfulness**

> As you are learning to become the observer of your thoughts and feelings. Notice how you can have more self-love. As you become more in tune with your own internal compass—your intuition—you can make life choices aligned with what makes you happy.

- **Act on what you need, rather than what you want**

> Sometimes what we want feeds the pleasure centers in our brain, but that pleasure is short-lived. Choose to act instead, based on your needs. Doing this will help you make choices that keep you centered, grounded and moving forward in life. By keeping your needs in focus, you can avoid the pitfalls of old patterns of behavior that get you stuck in a loop—like reaching for a glass of wine, or other compulsive behaviors.

- **Set healthy boundaries**

> Be authentically you. When you are in a place of self-love, you no longer need validation from others and you have a good sense of

what feels good and what doesn't.

  - Stay true to your character, your values and say no to the things that don't resonate or that deplete you physically, emotionally, mentally and spiritually.

- **Protect yourself and your energy**

  - Be careful who you allow into your life. Make sure they are aligned with who you're becoming and want only the best for you. There will always be people that take advantage, that engage in negative activities and don't wish you or others well because they themselves have not cultivated a strong sense of self-love. If you're doing all this work to be your best self, then keep your circle smaller. Protect your energy fiercely.

- **Learn to forgive—yourself and others**

  - Practice being more merciful with yourself. Holding onto negative emotions can be so harmful to the physical body and can send the spiritual, mental, and emotional bodies into disharmony.
  - Holding onto past resentment serves no one, especially you. Let it go and free yourself. Reset and flow higher.

TOOL #2: Meaning & Purpose

Primary Intervention for Spiritual / Energetic, Mental & Emotional bodies

Meaning is now widely recognized as essential to human well-being. As Baumeister has shown, *a happy life is impossible without meaning. A sense of meaning supports happiness.*

Remember, people who have discovered how to live a life of meaning get to enjoy numerous benefits, including greater happiness and wellbeing, higher life satisfaction, better control over their lives, and greater work satisfaction. They also experience fewer negative emotions, less anxiety and depression.

Simply put, "Other People Matter. Period," said Dr. Chris Peterson, one of the founding fathers of positive psychology. I will be the first person to say that most of this book has been about healing the self, but there is lightness and joy in getting outside ourselves and doing something to help others, even in some small way. For one thing, you can stop focusing on yourself and focus on how and why we are part of the world around us. Secondly, you can begin to see that even your complaints feel smaller as there are so many that are less blessed. When you practice helping others, how can you not sit with gratitude and count your blessings? Lastly, it will help you remember the interconnectedness of all things, including each other.

Remember that what gives you meaning is unique to you and your particular talents. If that wasn't proof enough that you belong, that you are worthy and special and uniquely talented with gifts to give to this world, then I don't know what is. Just let that sink in for a moment. YOU ARE UNIQUELY BLESSED WITH A TALENT that can help bring healing to yourself and others.

- Look at the times in your life when you felt happiest or most connected. Identify 3 or more of these moments and write every detail down about why you felt so excited, joyful, serene or happy.
- Identify your particular passion and/or talent that really lights you up. You may have more than one. If so, repeat this exercise for each one to see which of your talents you may want to work with.
- Find one or more ways to share this with others. It is your strength and talent that can bring others joy, ease or help in some way.
- Write down up to 3 ways to realign how you spend your time, so that you are living a life that truly gives you meaning and makes you feel like you're thriving!

TOOL #3:
Keep Your Vibration High

Primary Intervention for Spiritual / Energetic & Emotional Bodies

Secondary Bodies affected: Mental & Physical Bodies

As with the water experiments and Chladni's study of vibrations, our bodies respond to the vibrations we are exposed to, whether high or low. We get to choose if we want to entrain our body with love, healing, strength and passion and we get to choose what we expose ourselves to. Immerse your mind in positive energy and at least 70 percent of the matter in your body will synchronize with that elevated state.

If we focus our attention on remaining in an elevated state with positive emotions and thoughts, and we focus on our new outcomes, then we will find ourselves feeling lighter, happier and living life with more ease.

- Be consistent with your thoughts. Be consistent with your emotions. Be consistent with where you focus your attention. Where attention goes, energy flows. Consciously choose to stay in a peaceful, loving, abundant and powerful state of mind.
- If you feel yourself slipping into old ways of thinking and feeling, simply PAUSE & RESET TO KEEP YOUR VIBRATION HIGH.
- Go Bigger. Allow yourself to just expand your possibilities, expand your consciousness and imagine a life so elevated that you feel as though you're living a dream.
  - Expand on your Visualizations. Imagine an even bigger life than you could imagine right now. What would you be doing? What do you See, Hear and Feel in that moment?
  - Allow these moments to grow and expand more and more each day. You'll be delighted and amazed at what shows up.

The 6 Weeks to Happy Assessment

1. SLEEP QUALITY: 1☐ 2☐ 3☐
   Rate the quality of your sleep from 1 to 3, where 1 is Fair (less than 4 hours per night), 2 is Good (4 to 6 hours per night) and 3 is Great (7 or more hours per night)

2. TENSION IN THE BODY
   1☐ 2☐ 3☐

   Rate your level of tension in the body from 1 to 3, where 1 is Fair (breathing is labored, muscles are tight and tense in the neck and shoulders), 2 is Good (breathing is good, some tension in the neck and shoulders) and 3 is Great (breathing is relaxed and the body is no longer holding onto too much stress related tension)

3. ABILITY TO MANAGE ENERGY:
   1☐ 2☐ 3☐
   Rate your ability to manage and regulate your energy levels throughout the week, where 1 is Fair (very tired, not enough time and energy to do everything you need), 2 is Good (a bit tired, but getting better at prioritizing and managing your energy balance) and 3 is Great (sometimes tired, and overall doing well at re-prioritizing and making time to recharge)

4. ABILITY TO REGULATE MOOD & EMOTIONS:
   1☐ 2☐ 3☐
   Rate your ability to regulate your mood and emotions from 1 to 3, where 1 is Fair (irritable or easily agitated, short-tempered), 2 is Good (sometimes irritable or agitated), 3 is Great (able to choose your reactions more and stay calm)

5. STRESS LEVEL: 1☐ 2☐ 3☐
   Rate your stress level from 1 to 3, where 1 is Fair (moderate levels of worry, anxiety throughout the day), 2 is Good (low levels of worry and anxiety) and 3 is Great (knowing all is well and you're coping well)

6. FEELINGS OF HAPPINESS: 1☐ 2☐ 3☐
   Rate your feelings of happiness from 1 to 3, where 1 is Fair (infrequent feelings of hope, love, gratitude, joy, peace mixed with anxiety and worry), 2 is Good (frequent feelings of hope, love, gratitude, joy, peace) and 3 is Great (spending most of the day with feelings of happiness and a sense of grace and ease)

I hope that at the end of this six-week journey you have seen a shift toward the positive in your life and are now happily living with a greater sense of belonging, excitement, connection, love, gratitude, and abundance. Go forth and shine as you were meant to. Spread your wings and be your brilliant self!

I humbly thank you for allowing me to be your guide and look forward to hearing about your journey.

With love and light,

Zahra

ABOUT THE AUTHOR

Zahra Karsan

Author, Speaker, Certified Success Coach, Founder & CEO, GetZENd

Certified in Mindset Coaching and Neuroscience, Zahra is a public speaker as well as a trusted Success Coach to dozens of global executives. Voted by Yahoo Finance as a Top 10 Success Coach, she is the best-selling author of *How Do You TAKE YOUR HAPPY?* and the creator of the R.E.W.I.R.E System™, a groundbreaking methodology that retrains your brain for greater happiness, health, wealth and success. Her company, GetZEND, offers a suite of products that include online video training and an award-winning app to help you stay on track with your goals.

With over 20 years of experience as a Management Consultant and Corporate Coach, goal setting and producing results became second nature for Zahra. She now coaches corporations and industry leaders on how to achieve their life goals so they can live better. Most recently, Zahra Karsan was awarded a Top 100 Healthcare Visionaries Award by the International Forum for Advancements in Healthcare. She holds degrees in Psychology, Applied Positive Psychology, and Neuroscience, and holds certifications as a Master Neurolinguistic Programming Practitioner and Life Coach, Master Hypnotherapist and Master Timeline Therapy

Practitioner. She also continually endeavors to educate herself in the fields of Quantum and Metaphysics, and others, to bring you the latest research and most innovative tools so you can continue to thrive.

Zahra sits on the board of the World Happiness Foundation, whose mission is to create a world where we can be free, conscious, and happy. Zahra also works on her passion project with The Steve & Marjorie Harvey Foundation to empower young girls to move past limiting beliefs so they can live more powerfully.

RESOURCE CENTER

1. For more information on any of the services such as coaching, removal of negative emotions and limiting beliefs, how to reduce fear and self-doubt, or for additional resources, please visit **www.getzend.com.**
2. To download the GetZENd app to help you Relax, Focus and Perform Better, visit www.getzend.com, the Apple Store or at Google Play. Many of the tools and philosophies in this book have been built into the GetZENd app. If you are new to mindfulness, meditation or would like performance made easy, then try the app and let it guide you.
3. For upcoming workshops or to go deeper with this work, please sign up for our newsletter at www.getzend.com.
4. For future speaking events and upcoming training, please visit www.getzend.com. We will keep the website updated with the latest research, blogs, and events. Stay with us and stay tuned in!
5. Follow us on social media. See the links below or go to www.getzend.com for the latest handles.
    - > Instagram: @successcoachzara
    - > Instagram: @getzend
    - > Facebook @getzend
    - > LinkedIN: Zahra Karsan
6. Look for us in the App Store and on Google Play as we continue to update and bring you the latest and greatest technology to help you R.E.W.I.R.E so you can relax, focus, perform better, and live a happier life. Just type GetZENd in the App Store or search for it at Google Play.

BIBLIOGRAPHY

Articles

Dusek, J. A., et al. 2008: "Stress management versus lifestyle modification on systolic hypertension and medication elimination: A randomized trial", *The Journal of Alternative and Complementary Medicine*, 14, 129-138.

Elder, Charles et al. "Effect of transcendental meditation on employee stress, depression, and burnout: a randomized controlled study." *The Permanente journal* vol. 18,1 (2014): 19-23. doi:10.7812/TPP/13-102. https://www.ncbi.nlm.nih.gov/pmc/articles/PMC3951026/.

Goyal M, Singh S, Sibinga EMS, et al. Meditation Programs for Psychological Stress and Well-being: A Systematic Review and Meta-analysis. *JAMA Intern Med.* 2014;174(3):357–368. doi:10.1001/jamainternmed.2013.13018. https://jamanetwork.com/journals/jamainternalmedicine/fullarticle/1809754.

Goldin, Philippe et al. "Mindfulness Meditation Training and Self-Referential Processing in Social Anxiety Disorder: Behavioral and Neural Effects." *Journal of cognitive psychotherapy* vol. 23,3 (2009): 242-257. doi:10.1891/0889-8391.23.3.242.

Britta K. Hölzel, James Carmody, Mark Vangel, Christina Congleton, Sita M. Yerramsetti, Tim Gard, Sara W. Lazar, Mindfulness practice leads to increases in regional brain gray matter density, Psychiatry Research: Neuroimaging, Volume 191, Issue 1, 2011, Pages 36-43, ISSN 0925-4927, https://doi.org/10.1016/j.pscychresns.2010.08.006. https://www.sciencedirect.com/science/article/abs/pii/S092549271000288X.

Lazar, S. W., Kerr, C. E., Wasserman, R. H., Gray, J. R., Greve, D. N., Treadway, M. T., ... & Fischl, B. (2005). "Meditation experience is associated with increased cortical thickness." *Neuroreport*, 16(17), 1893.

Walsh, R., & Shapiro, S. L. (2006). "The meeting of meditative disciplines and western psychology: A mutually enriching dialogue." *American Psychologist*, 61(3), 227–239. https://doi.org/10.1037/0003-066X.61.3.227.

Daphne M. Davis, Ph.D., and Jeffrey A. Hayes Ph.D., "What are the benefits of mindfulness?", *American Psychological Association,* July/August 2012, Vol 43, No. 7, Print version: page 64.

Chambers, R., Lo, B.C.Y. & Allen, N.B. The Impact of Intensive Mindfulness Training on Attentional Control, Cognitive Style, and Affect. Cogn Ther Res 32, 303–322 (2008). https://doi.org/10.1007/s10608-007-9119-0.

Hofmann SG, Sawyer AT, Witt AA, Oh D. The effect of mindfulness-based therapy on anxiety and depression: A meta-analytic review. *J Consult Clin Psychol.* 2010;78(2):169-183. doi:10.1037/a0018555.

Farb, Norman A S et al. "Minding one's emotions: mindfulness training alters the neural expression of sadness." *Emotion* (*Washington,* D.C.) vol. 10,1 (2010): 25-33. doi:10.1037/a0017151.

Jha AP, Stanley EA, Kiyonaga A, Wong L, Gelfand L. Examining the protective effects of mindfulness training on working memory capacity and affective experience. *Emotion*. 2010 Feb;10(1):54-64. doi: 10.1037/a0018438. PMID: 20141302.

Moore A, Malinowski P. Meditation, mindfulness and cognitive flexibility. *Conscious Cogn*. 2009 Mar.18(1):176-86. doi: 10.1016/j.concog.2008.12.008. Epub 2009 Jan 31. PMID: 19181542.

Ortner, C. N. M., Kilner, S. J., & Zelazo, P. D. (2007). Mindfulness meditation and reduced emotional interference on a cognitive task. *Motivation and Emotion*, 31(4), 271-283. https://doi.org/10.1007/s11031-007-9076-7.

Siegel, Daniel J.. "Mindfulness training and neural integration: differentiation of distinct streams of awareness and the cultivation of well-being." *Social cognitive and affective neuroscience* vol. 2,4 (2007): 259–263. doi:10.1093/scan/nsm034.

Cahn, B. R., & Polich, J. (2006). Meditation states and traits: EEG, ERP, and neuroimaging studies. Psychological Bulletin, 132(2), 180–211. https://doi.org/10.1037/0033-2909.132.2.180.

Davidson, R. J., Jackson, D. C., & Kalin, N. H. (2000). Emotion, plasticity, context, and regulation: Perspectives from affective neuroscience. *Psychological Bulletin*, 126(6), 890–909. https://doi.org/10.1037/0033-2909.126.6.890.

Barnes S, Brown KW, Krusemark E, Campbell WK, Rogge RD. The role of mindfulness in romantic relationship satisfaction and responses to relationship stress. *J Marital Fam Ther.* 2007 Oct;33(4):482-500. doi: 10.1111/j.1752-0606.2007.00033.x. PMID: 17935531.

Dekeyser, M., Raes, F., Leijssen, M., Leysen, S., & Dewulf, D. (2008). Mindfulness skills and interpersonal behavior. *Personality and Individual Differences*, 44(5), 1235–1245. https://doi.org/10.1016/j.paid.2007.11.018.

Wachs, K., & Cordova, J. V. (2007). Mindful relating: Exploring mindfulness and emotion repertoires in intimate relationships. *Journal of Marital and Family Therapy*, 33(4), 464–481. https://doi.org/10.1111/j.1752-0606.2007.00032.x

Davidson RJ, Kabat-Zinn J, Schumacher J, Rosenkranz M, Muller D, Santorelli SF, Urbanowski F, Harrington A, Bonus K, Sheridan JF. Alterations in brain and immune function produced by mindfulness meditation. *Psychosom Med.* 2003 Jul-Aug;65(4):564-70. doi: 10.1097/01.psy.0000077505.67574.e3. PMID: 12883106.

Grossman P, Niemann L, Schmidt S, Walach H. Mindfulness-based stress reduction and health benefits. A meta-analysis. *J Psychosom Res.* 2004 Jul;57(1):35-43. doi: 10.1016/S0022-3999(03)00573-7. PMID: 15256293.

Carmody J, Baer RA. Relationships between mindfulness practice and levels of mindfulness, medical and psychological symptoms and well-being in a mindfulness-based stress reduction program. *J Behav Med.*

2008 Feb;31(1):23-33. doi: 10.1007/s10865-007-9130-7. Epub 2007 Sep 25. PMID: 17899351.

Coffey, K. A., & Hartman, M. (2008). Mechanisms of action in the inverse relationship between mindfulness and psychological distress. *Complementary Health Practice Review*, 13(2), 79–91. https://doi.org/10.1177/1533210108316307

Ostafin, B. D., Chawla, N., Bowen, S., Dillworth, T. M., Witkiewitz, K., & Marlatt, G. A. (2006). Intensive Mindfulness Training and the Reduction of Psychological Distress: A Preliminary Study. Cognitive and Behavioral Practice, 13(3), 191–197. https://doi.org/10.1016/j.cbpra.2005.12.001.

Lutz A, Slagter HA, Rawlings NB, Francis AD, Greischar LL, Davidson RJ. Mental training enhances attentional stability: neural and behavioral evidence. *J Neurosci.* 2009 Oct 21;29(42):13418-27. doi: 10.1523/JNEUROSCI.1614-09.2009. PMID: 19846729; PMCID: PMC2789281.

Davidson, Richard J, and Antoine Lutz. "Buddha's Brain: Neuroplasticity and Meditation." *IEEE signal processing magazine* vol. 25,1 (2008): 176-174. doi:10.1109/msp.2008.4431873.

Rollin McCraty, Ph.D. Mike Atkinson, and Dana Tomasino, B.A. *Modulation of DNA Conformation by Heart-Focused Intention.* Heartmath.org. 2003. Accessed June, 2021. https://www.aipro.info/drive/File/224.pdf.

Radin D, Hayssen G, Emoto M, Kizu T. Double-blind test of the effects of distant intention on water crystal formation. Explore (NY). 2006 Sep-Oct;2(5):408-11. doi: 10.1016/j.explore.2006.06.004. PMID: 16979104.

Hanson, J.A. and VanderWeele, T.J., The Comprehensive Measure of Meaning: psychological and philosophical foundations. In: M. Lee, L.D. Kubzansky, and T.J. VanderWeele (Eds.). Measuring Well-Being: Interdisciplinary Perspectives from the Social Sciences and the Humanities.

Oxford University Press, forthcoming. https://cdn1.sph.harvard.edu/wp-content/uploads/sites/603/2020/01/ComprehensiveMeasureMeaning.pdf.

Steger, M. F. (2009). *Meaning in life.* In S. J. Lopez (Ed.), Oxford handbook of positive psychology (2nd ed., pp. 679-687). Oxford: Oxford University Press.

George, L. S., & Park, C. L. (2013). Are meaning and purpose distinct? An examination of correlates and predictors. *The Journal of Positive Psychology, 8*(5), 365–375. https://doi.org/10.1080/17439760.2013.805801

Mcknight, Patrick & Kashdan, Todd. (2009). Purpose in Life as a System That Creates and Sustains Health and Well-Being: An Integrative, Testable Theory. Review of General Psychology – REV GEN PSYCHOL. 13. 10.1037/a0017152.

Books

Baumeister and Tierney. *Willpower: Rediscovering the Greatest Human Strength*

Chapman, Gary. *The 5 Love Languages*

Church, Dawson. *Mind over Matter*

Dispenza, Dr. Joe. *Becoming Supernatural: How Common People Are Doing The Uncommon*

Frankl, Victor. *Man's Search for Meaning*

Baumeister, Roy F. *Meanings of Life*

Guillebeau, Chris. *The Happiness of Pursuit*

Hanson, Dr. Rick. *Hardwiring Happiness*

Links

Tris Thorp. Daily Practices for Spiritual, Mental, Emotional, and Physical Well-being. April 2019. Accessed June 2021. https://chopra.com/articles/daily-practices-for-spiritual-mental-emotional-and-physical-well-being

Neuroplasticity. The Sentis Brain Animation Series. Nov. 2012. Accessed April 2021.

https://www.youtube.com/watch?v=ELpfYCZa87g.

Topor, David R. Ph.D., MS-HPEd. *If you are happy and you know it... you may live longer.* Dec. 2019. Accessed June 2021.https://www.health.harvard.edu/blog/if-you-are-happy-and-you-know-it-you-may-live-longer-2019101618020.

Lawler, Moira. Learn about mindfulness and its benefits—and how to practice it with or without meditation. Insider.com. May 2020. Accessed June 2021. https://www.insider.com/what-is-mindfulness.

Journey Pure. https://journeypure.com/about-us/.

Cairns, Rebecca. Insider.com. *What is meditation? How the popular wellness practice can benefit you.* June 2020. Accessed April 2021. https://www.insider.com/what-is-meditation.

Cerretani, Jessica. Harvard Medicine Magazine. *The Contagion of Happiness.* Spring, 2021. https://hms.harvard.edu/magazine/science-emotion/contagion-happiness.

Johnston, Ken. *The Olympics, then...now...and the Edge.* Fresh Air Creating Positive Change Blog. Feb. 2010. Accessed June 2021. http://freshairecreatingpositivechange.blogspot.com/2010/02/olympics-thennowand-edge.html

Zhivotsovkaya, Emiliya. *Certificate Applied Positive Psychology,* The Flourishing Centre. https://theflourishingcenter.com/capp/.

Lino, Catarina. *Positive Psychology Theory in a Nutshell.* Dec. 2020. Accessed June 2021. https://positivepsychology.com/positive-psychology-theory/.

Peterson, Christopher Ph.D. *Other People Matter: Two Examples.* Psychologytoday.com. June 2008. Accessed, June 2021. https://www.psychologytoday.com/us/blog/the-good-life/200806/other-people-matter-two-examples?amp=

Ackerman, Courtney E., MA. *What is Self-Compassion and what is Self-Love?* Positivepsychology.com. Oct. 2020. Accessed June 2021. https://positivepsychology.com/self-compassion-self-love/.

Nortje, Alicia Ph.D. "Realizing Your Meaning: 5 Ways to Live a Meaningful Life", Positivepsychology.com, May 2021. Accessed June 2021. https://positivepsychology.com/live-meaningful-life/.

Other Resources

Lamott, Anne. *Anne Lamott Quotes* (Author of Bird by Bird). N.p., n.d. Web. 04 Apr. 2017.

Brown, Brene. *The Gifts of Imperfection: Let Go of Who You Think You're Supposed to Be and Embrace Who You Are. Center City*, MN: Hazelden, 2010. Print.

Coelho, Paulo, and Alan Clarke. *The Alchemist.* New York: HarperCollins, 1993. Print.

Dienstmann, Giovanni. "76 Scientific Benefits of Meditation." *Live and Dare.* Giovanni Dienstmann, 22 Jan. 2017. Web. 04 Apr. 2017.

Dispenza, Joe, and Daniel G. Amen. *Breaking the Habit of Being Yourself: How to Lose Your Mind and Create a New One.* Carlsbad, CA: Hay House, 2015. Print.

Guillebeau, Chris. *Happiness of Pursuit: Finding the Quest That Will Bring Purpose to Your Life.* New York: Harmony, 2016. Print.

Hanson, Rick. *Hardwiring Happiness: The New Brain Science of Contentment, Calm, and Confidence.* New York: Harmony Crown, 2016. Print.

James, Tad, and Wyatt Lee Woodsmall. *Time Line Therapy and the Basis of Personality.* Cupertino, CA: Meta Publications, 1988. Print.

Lewis, Byron A., and R. Frank. Pucelik. *Magic of NLP Demystified.* Bancyfelin: Crown House, 2012. Print.

Team, Brain And Spine. Wanna Give? This Is Your Brain on a 'Helper's High'. *Health Essentials from Cleveland Clinic.* N.p., 18 Nov. 2016. Web. 04 Apr. 2017.

Wong, Sam. Ballet dancers' brains adapt to stop them feeling dizzy. Imperial College London, 27 Sept 2013, retrieved from https://www.imperial.ac.uk/news/130786/ballet-dancers-brains-adapt-stop-them/

Formica, Michael J, Neuroplasticity: The Revolution in Neuroscience and Psychology, Part I The science of change, *Psychology Today*, 30 Jun 2008, retrieved from https://www.psychologytoday.com/us/blog/enlightened-living/200806/neuroplasticity-the-revolution-in-neuroscience-and-psychology-part-i

Brann, A, 5 Neuroplasticity Exercises All Coaches Should Know, Neuroscience for Coaches, 21 Jan 2016 retrieved from http://neuroscienceforcoaches.com/n4c-blog/5-neuroplasticity-exercises/

Yoon, Kyung Jae; Oh, Byung-Mo; Kim , Dae-Yul, Functional improvement and neuroplastic effects of anodal transcranial direct current stimulation (tdcs) delivered 1 day vs. 1 week after cerebral ischemia in rats, Brain research, 2012, Vol.1452, pp.61-72

Ackerman, Courtney. What is Neuroplasticity?, *Positive Psychology Program*, 25 July 2018, retrieved from https://positivepsychologyprogram.com/neuroplasticity/

Lane, Earl. Experts Describe Long-Term Impacts of Stress on the Young Brain, American Association for the Advancement of Science, 16

Jul 2013, retrieved from https://www.aaas.org/news/experts-describe-long-term-impacts-stress-young-brain

Brenner, Sharon; Jones, John P; Muehlenbein, Michael P; Rutanen-Whaley, Riitta H; Parker, William; Flinn, Mark V, Evolutionary Mismatch and Chronic Psychological Stress, *Research Gate*, Jan 2015 retrieved from https://www.researchgate.net/publication/276433796_Evolutionary_Mismatch_and_Chronic_Psychological_Stress

Krantz, David S; Thorn, Beverly; Kiecolt-Glaser, Janice, *How Stress Affects Your Health*, Revised 2013, retrieved from https://www.apa.org/helpcenter/stress.aspx

Stress Effects, *The American Institute of Stress*, 20 Sept 2018, retrieved from https://www.stress.org/stress-effects/

Pal, Parneet, Battling the Physical Symptoms of Stress, *Harvard Business Review*, 23 Jun 2016, retrieved from https://hbr.org/2016/06/battling-the-physical-symptoms-of-stress

Keller, Abiola; Litzelman, Kristin; Wisk, Lauren; Maddox, Torsheika; Cheng, Erika Rose; Creswell, Paul D; Witt, Whitney P., Does the Perception that Stress Affects Health Matter? *The Association with Health and Mortality*, US National Library of Medicine National Institutes of Health, 1 Sep 2013, retrieved from https://www.ncbi.nlm.nih.gov/pmc/articles/PMC3374921/

Racco, Marilisa, This is the state of stress in 2018, Global News, 16 April 2018 retrieved from https://globalnews.ca/news/4138006/stress-causes-today/

Jabr, Ferris, Cache Cab: Taxi Drivers' Brains Grow to Navigate London's Streets, *Scientific American*, 8 Dec 2011, retrieved from https://www.bbc.com/news/health-16086233

Maguire, EA; Woollett, K; Spiers, HJ; London taxi drivers and bus drivers: a structural MRI and neuropsychological analysis, *US National Library of Medicine National Institues of Health*, 2016, retrieved from https://www.ncbi.nlm.nih.gov/pubmed/17024677

ENDNOTES

1 Daily Practices for Spiritual, Mental, Emotional, and Physical Well-being. April, 2019. Accessed June, 2021. https://chopra.com/articles/daily-practices-for-spiritual-mental-emotional-and-physical-well-being.

2 The Sentis Brain Animation Series. *Neuroplasticity*. Nov., 2012. Accessed April, 2021.https://www.youtube.com/watch?v=ELpfYCZa87g.

3 If you are happy and you know it… you may live longer. Dec, 2019. Accessed June, 2021.https://www.health.harvard.edu/blog/if-you-are-happy-and-you-know-it-you-may-live-longer-2019101618020.

4 Dusek, J. A., et al. 2008: Stress management versus lifestyle modification on systolic hypertension and medication elimination: A randomized trial, T*he Journal of Alternative and Complementary Medicine*, 14, 129-138.

5 Heger, E. (2020, June 22). 7 Benefits of Meditation, and How it Can Affect Your Brain. Insider. https://www.insider.com/benefits-of-meditation. Quoted by David Foley, David Foley, founder of Unify Cosmos, a meditation center in Oklahoma.

6 Elder, Charles et al. "Effect of transcendental meditation on employee stress, depression, and burnout: a randomized controlled study." T*he Permanente journal* vol. 18,1 (2014): 19-23. doi:10.7812/TPP/13-102https://www.ncbi.nlm.nih.gov/pmc/articles/PMC3951026/

7 Goyal M, Singh S, Sibinga EMS, et al. Meditation Programs for Psychological Stress and Well-being: A Systematic Review and Meta-analysis. *JAMA Intern Med.* 2014;174(3):357–368. doi:10.1001/jamainternmed.2013.13018. https://jamanetwork.com/journals/jamainternalmedicine/fullarticle/1809754.

8 Goldin, Philippe et al. "Mindfulness Meditation Training and Self-Referential Processing in Social Anxiety Disorder: Behavioral and Neural Effects." *Journal of cognitive psychotherapy* vol. 23,3 (2009): 242-257. doi:10.1891/0889-8391.23.3.242.

9 Lawler, Moira.Learn about mindfulness and its benefits—and how to practice it with or without meditation. Insider.com. May, 2020. Accessed June, 2021. https://www.insider.com/what-is-mindfulness.

10 Britta K. Hölzel, James Carmody, Mark Vangel, Christina Congleton, Sita M. Yerramsetti, Tim Gard, Sara W. Lazar, Mindfulness practice leads to increases in regional brain gray matter density, Psychiatry Research: Neuroimaging, Volume 191, Issue 1, 2011, Pages 36-43, ISSN 0925-4927, https://doi.org/10.1016/j.pscychresns.2010.08.006. https://www.sciencedirect.com/science/article/abs/pii/S092549271000288X.

11 Lazar, S. W., Kerr, C. E., Wasserman, R. H., Gray, J. R., Greve, D. N., Treadway, M. T., ... & Fischl, B. (2005). "Meditation experience is associated with increased cortical thickness." *Neuroreport,* 16(17), 1893.

12 Walsh, R., & Shapiro, S. L. (2006). "The meeting of meditative disciplines and western psychology: A mutually enriching dialogue." *American Psychologist,* 61(3), 227–239. https://doi.org/10.1037/0003-066X.61.3.227.

13 *What are the benefits of mindfulness?* By Daphne M. Davis, PhD, and Jeffrey A. Hayes, PhD, July/August 2012, Vol 43, No. 7, Print version: page 64.

14 https://journeypure.com/about-us/

15 Chambers, R., Lo, B.C.Y. & Allen, N.B. The Impact of Intensive Mindfulness Training on Attentional Control, Cognitive Style, and Affect. Cogn Ther Res 32, 303–322 (2008). https://doi.org/10.1007/s10608-007-9119-0.

16 Hofmann SG, Sawyer AT, Witt AA, Oh D. The effect of mindfulness-based therapy on anxiety and depression: A meta-analytic review. *J Consult Clin Psychol.* 2010;78(2):169-183. doi:10.1037/a0018555.

17 Farb, Norman A S et al. "Minding one's emotions: mindfulness training alters the neural expression of sadness." *Emotion (Washington, D.C.)* vol. 10,1 (2010): 25-33. doi:10.1037/a0017151.

18 Ibid.

19 Jha AP, Stanley EA, Kiyonaga A, Wong L, Gelfand L. Examining the protective effects of mindfulness training on working memory capacity and affective experience. *Emotion.* 2010 Feb;10(1):54-64. doi: 10.1037/a0018438. PMID: 20141302.

20 Moore A, Malinowski P. Meditation, mindfulness and cognitive flexibility. Conscious Cogn. 2009 Mar;18(1):176-86. doi: 10.1016/j.concog.2008.12.008. Epub 2009 Jan 31. PMID: 19181542.

21 Ortner, C. N. M., Kilner, S. J., & Zelazo, P. D. (2007). Mindfulness meditation and reduced emotional interference on a cognitive task. *Moti-*

vation and Emotion, 31(4), 271-283. https://doi.org/10.1007/s11031-007-9076-7.

22 Siegel, Daniel J. "Mindfulness training and neural integration: differentiation of distinct streams of awareness and the cultivation of well-being." *Social cognitive and affective neuroscience* vol. 2,4 (2007): 259–263. doi:10.1093/scan/nsm034.

23 Cahn, B. R., & Polich, J. (2006). Meditation states and traits: EEG, ERP, and neuroimaging studies. *Psychological Bulletin*, 132(2), 180–211. https://doi.org/10.1037/0033-2909.132.2.180.

24 Davidson, R. J., Jackson, D. C., & Kalin, N. H. (2000). Emotion, plasticity, context, and regulation: Perspectives from affective neuroscience. Psychological Bulletin, 126(6), 890–909. https://doi.org/10.1037/0033-2909.126.6.890.

25 Barnes S, Brown KW, Krusemark E, Campbell WK, Rogge RD. The role of mindfulness in romantic relationship satisfaction and responses to relationship stress. *J Marital Fam Ther.* 2007 Oct;33(4):482-500. doi: 10.1111/j.1752-0606.2007.00033.x. PMID: 17935531.

26 Dekeyser, M., Raes, F., Leijssen, M., Leysen, S., & Dewulf, D. (2008). Mindfulness skills and interpersonal behaviour. Personality and Individual Differences, 44(5), 1235–1245. https://doi.org/10.1016/j.paid.2007.11.018.

27 Wachs, K., & Cordova, J. V. (2007). Mindful relating: Exploring mindfulness and emotion repertoires in intimate relationships. *Journal of Marital and Family Therapy*, 33(4), 464–481. https://doi.org/10.1111/j.1752-0606.2007.00032.x.

28 Davidson RJ, Kabat-Zinn J, Schumacher J, Rosenkranz M, Muller D, Santorelli SF, Urbanowski F, Harrington A, Bonus K, Sheridan JF. Alterations in brain and immune function produced by mindfulness meditation. *Psychosom Med.* 2003 Jul-Aug;65(4):564-70. doi: 10.1097/01.psy.0000077505.67574.e3. PMID: 12883106.

29 Grossman P, Niemann L, Schmidt S, Walach H. Mindfulness-based stress reduction and health benefits. A meta-analysis. *J Psychosom* Res. 2004 Jul;57(1):35-43. doi: 10.1016/S0022-3999(03)00573-7. PMID: 15256293.

30 Carmody J, Baer RA. Relationships between mindfulness practice and levels of mindfulness, medical and psychological symptoms and well-being in a mindfulness-based stress reduction program. *J Behav Med.* 2008 Feb;31(1):23-33. doi: 10.1007/s10865-007-9130-7. Epub 2007 Sep 25.

PMID: 17899351.

31 Coffey, K. A., & Hartman, M. (2008). Mechanisms of action in the inverse relationship between mindfulness and psychological distress. *Complementary Health Practice Review*, 13(2), 79–91. https://doi.org/10.1177/1533210108316307.

32 Ostafin, B. D., Chawla, N., Bowen, S., Dillworth, T. M., Witkiewitz, K., & Marlatt, G. A. (2006). Intensive Mindfulness Training and the Reduction of Psychological Distress: A Preliminary Study. Cognitive and Behavioral Practice, 13(3), 191–197. https://doi.org/10.1016/j.cbpra.2005.12.001.

33 Moore A, Malinowski P. Meditation, mindfulness and cognitive flexibility. Conscious Cogn. 2009 Mar;18(1):176-86. doi: 10.1016/j.concog.2008.12.008. Epub 2009 Jan 31. PMID: 19181542.

34 Lutz A, Slagter HA, Rawlings NB, Francis AD, Greischar LL, Davidson RJ. Mental training enhances attentional stability: neural and behavioral evidence. *J Neurosci*. 2009 Oct 21;29(42):13418-27. doi: 10.1523/JNEUROSCI.1614-09.2009. PMID: 19846729; PMCID: PMC2789281.

35 Cairns, Rebecca. Insider.com. *What is meditation? How the popular wellness practice can benefit you*. June, 2020. Accessed April, 2021. https://www.insider.com/what-is-meditation.

36 Davidson, Richard J, and Antoine Lutz. "Buddha's Brain: Neuroplasticity and Meditation." *IEEE signal processing magazine* vol. 25,1 (2008): 176-174. doi:10.1109/msp.2008.4431873.

37 Baumeister and Tierney. Willpower: *Rediscovering the Greatest Human Strength*. Penguin Books; Reprint edition (August 28, 2012).

38 Cerretani, Jessica. Harvard Medicine Magazine. T*he Contagion of Happiness*. Spring, 2021. https://hms.harvard.edu/magazine/science-emotion/contagion-happiness.

39 Chapman, Gary. *The 5 Love Languages*. Northfield Publishing; Reprint edition 2014.

40 Hanson, D. R. (2015). Hardwiring Happiness. Random House USA.

41 Johnston, Ken. The Olympics, then...now...and the Edge. Fresh Air Creating Positive Change Blog. Feb., 2010. Accessed June, 2021. http://freshairecreatingpositivechange.blogspot.com/2010/02/olympics-then-nowand-edge.html

42 Dispenza, D. J. (2017). Becoming Supernatural: How Common People

are Doing the Uncommon. Hay House, Inc.

43 Church, D. (2018). Mind to matter: The Astonishing Science of How Your Brain Creates Material Reality. Hay House.

44 Rollin McCraty, Ph.D. Mike Atkinson, and Dana Tomasino, B.A. *Modulation of DNA Conformation by Heart-Focused Intention.* Heartmath.org. 2003. Accessed June, 2021. https://www.aipro.info/drive/File/224.pdf.

45 Tolle, E. (2018). A New Earth: Awakening to Your Life's Purpose. Penguin Books.

46 Richards, S. (2006). Cosmic Ordering Guide: Where Dreams Can Become Reality! Mirage.

47 Church, D. (2014). Genie in Your Genes: Epigenetic Medicine and The New Biology of Intention. Energy Psychology Press.

48 Radin D, Hayssen G, Emoto M, Kizu T. Double-blind test of the effects of distant intention on water crystal formation. Explore (NY). 2006 Sep-Oct;2(5):408-11. doi: 10.1016/j.explore.2006.06.004. PMID: 16979104.

49 Church, D. (2018). Mind to matter: The Astonishing Science of How Your Brain Creates Material Reality. Hay House.

50 Hanson, J.A. and VanderWeele, T.J., The Comprehensive Measure of Meaning: psychological and philosophical foundations. In: M. Lee, L.D. Kubzansky, and T.J. VanderWeele (Eds.). Measuring Well-Being: Interdisciplinary Perspectives from the Social Sciences and the Humanities. *Oxford University Press,* forthcoming. https://cdn1.sph.harvard.edu/wp-content/uploads/sites/603/2020/01/ComprehensiveMeasureMeaning.pdf.

51 Steger, M. F. (2009). Meaning in life. In S. J. Lopez (Ed.), Oxford handbook of positive psychology (2nd ed., pp. 679-687). Oxford: Oxford University Press.

52 Certificate Applied Positive Psychology, The Flourishing Centre. Emiliya Zhivotsovkaya. https://theflourishingcenter.com/capp/.

53 George, L. S., & Park, C. L. (2013). Are meaning and purpose distinct? An examination of correlates and predictors. *The Journal of Positive Psychology,* 8(5), 365–375. https://doi.org/10.1080/17439760.2013.805801

54 Lino, Catarina. *Positive Psychology Theory in a Nutshell.* Positivepsychology.com. Dec, 2020. Accessed June, 2021.

https://positivepsychology.com/positive-psychology-theory/.

55 Peterson, Christopher Ph.D. *Other People Matter: Two Examples.* Psychologytoday.com. June, 2008. Accessed, June, 2021. https://www.psychologytoday.com/us/blog/the-good-life/200806/other-people-matter-two-examples?amp=

56 Ackerman, Courtney E., MA. *What is Self-Compassion and what is Self-Love?* Positivepsychology.com. Oct., 2020. Accessed June, 2021. https://positivepsychology.com/self-compassion-self-love/

57 Khoshaba, D. (2012, March 27). A Seven-Step Prescription for Self-Love. Psychology Today. https://www.psychologytoday.com/us/blog/get-hardy/201203/seven-step-prescription-self-love.

58 Mcknight, Patrick & Kashdan, Todd. (2009). Purpose in Life as a System That Creates and Sustains Health and Well-Being: An Integrative, Testable Theory. Review of General Psychology - REV GEN PSYCHOL. 13. 10.1037/a0017152.

59 Nortje, Alicia Ph.D. "Realizing Your Meaning: 5 Ways to Live a Meaningful Life", Positivepsychology.com, May, 2021. Accessed June, 2021. https://positivepsychology.com/live-meaningful-life/.

60 Kröplin, P. D. B., & Henschel, R. C. (2017). Water and its Memory: New Astonishing Insights in Water Research. AT Verlag; 1. Auflage.

61 Cairns, Rebecca. Insider.com. *What is meditation? How the popular wellness practice can benefit you.* June, 2020. Accessed April, 2021. https://www.insider.com/what-is-meditation.

Made in the USA
Las Vegas, NV
20 December 2021

38932097R00134